THE SAMURAI
WARRIOR

The SAMURAI WARRIOR

THE GOLDEN AGE OF JAPAN'S ELITE WARRIORS
1560–1615

BEN HUBBARD

METRO BOOKS
New York

METRO BOOKS
New York

An Imprint of Sterling Publishing
387 Park Avenue South
New York, NY 10016

Editorial and design by
Amber Books Ltd
74–77 White Lion Street
London N1 9PF
www.amberbooks.co.uk

Project Editor: Michael Spilling
Designer: Zoë Mellors
Picture Research: Terry Forshaw

ISBN: 978-1-4351-5374-5

For information about custom editions, special sales, and premium and corporate purchases,
please contact Sterling Special Sales at 800-805-5489 or specialsales@sterlingpublishing.com.

Manufactured in China

2 4 6 8 10 9 7 5 3 1

www.sterlingpublishing.com

Introduction

The period of Japanese history between 1550 and 1615 is often considered something of a golden era for the samurai. This is when the warriors reached the zenith of their powers and united the country under the sword. This in turn led Japan into a new epoch, where samurai underlings could rise through the ranks and become powerful leaders.

These warlords would then crush and conquer any clan that opposed them using the latest breakthrough in weapons technology – the arquebus. When the smoke cleared, Japan entered an enforced period of peace that would last for over 250 years. But this peace would also herald the beginning of the end for the samurai, who without wars to fight became an irrelevant burden on the feudal society they had created.

The samurai first began as eighth-century warriors hired by the Emperor to subdue native 'barbarians' who harassed the empire's furthest

Facing page: A fourteenth-century century scroll depicts a dramatic battle between Minamoto and Taira samurai at the Rokuhara mansion in Kyoto.

Right: Early samurai combat consisted of a mounted archery duel between two warriors of equal rank. A swordfight on the ground would often follow.

frontiers. Their battles were often skirmishes fought at close quarters, and the warriors' long, straight, thrusting sword proved utterly useless against them. Instead, the Emperor's men had to adopt the fighting methods of the natives they were charged with subduing. This meant mounted duels with bows and arrows, and swords cast with a special curved edge for slashing at opponents on horseback.

Soul of the Samurai

This sword would later become the mighty katana, often called the 'soul of the samurai'. Considered a spiritual extension of the warrior himself, the katana was a masterpiece of sword-making. The genius of the blade lay in its bimetallic makeup – a hard cutting edge wrapped around a soft, flexible core. A samurai's katana would only leave his side in death and even after the warrior order had ceased to exist the sword

宇治
之
戦

Above: The Battle of Uji signalled the start of the Gempei War between the Minamoto and Taira clans. Here, naginata-wielding warrior monks stop the Taira from crossing Uji Bridge.

battle was expected to commit seppuku, or suicide by slitting open the stomach, as a matter of honour. To an extent, early battles between samurai warriors were considered an honourable exchange. They would start when one mounted warrior called out his rank, family name and achievements to attract an enemy warrior of similar standing. The ensuing archery duel was therefore viewed as consensual combat between gentlemen. Sometimes the foot soldiers fighting around these gentlemen warriors would even take a consensual pause and halt proceedings to admire a particularly heroic bout.

But this would all change in the mid-sixteenth century when a new weapon that washed up on Japanese shores would challenge notions of honour and heroism in battle. This was the arquebus, a matchlock firearm that arrived on board a shipwrecked Portuguese trading boat. The weapon was of enormous interest to samurai warlords known as daimyō, the leaders of the warring samurai clans that now made up Japan. Known as the Sengoku Jidai, or the 'Age of the Country at War', this was a period of great upheaval. Many centuries previously the Emperor had his power wrested from his control by the Shōgun, the 'barbarian-subduing commander-in-chief' tasked with protecting him. But over time the Shōgun's position too had weakened. Now, titles were all but meaningless in the face of the burgeoning military might of the daimyōs.

The sixteenth century rise of the daimyōs was the first time in samurai history that a warlord without aristocratic blood could seize power and rule over

continued to be a symbol of the samurai ethos. Bushidō, or 'Way of the Warrior', was the samurai's code of ethics, which enshrined loyalty, honour, fearlessness, honesty and self-sacrifice. Brave warriors would display their bushidō virtues on the battlefield, or die trying. Any samurai defeated in

CONTENTS

Japan. This was so extraordinary that it even had its own name: gekokujō, or 'the low overcomes the high.' One of the most famous cases of gekokujō was Oda Nobunaga (1534–82), also known as the first great unifier of Japan. Nobunaga was a young upstart who took great risks in war and won the ultimate reward: domination of the country and the majority of the clans that opposed him. Nobunaga's rapid and often brutal ascendancy to power was aided in no small part by the arquebus. Unlike some of his more gentlemanly rivals, who used the gun as an auxiliary weapon from their back lines, Nobunaga made the arquebus the central element of his armies. He first put the weapon to devastating use in the 1575 Battle of Nagashino. Here, protected by palisades, three frontlines of warriors delivered rotating volleys of arquebus fire to mow down the enemy's charges. After this assault, samurai were able to slip through gaps in the palisades and finish off any survivors with their swords.

Right: Kusunoki Masashige's statue stands guard outside Tokyo's Imperial Palace. Masashige immortalized himself by leading an army into a battle he knew could not be won.

The End of Honour

News of the battle astounded samurai veterans. It was a shock to think that Nobunaga's sudden supremacy had apparently come to pass because of the arquebus. The weapon itself was considered to be offensive and dishonourable by bushidō purists. Here was a weapon that a lowly foot soldier could learn to use in a day to take down a mounted

samurai gentlemen who had spent his life training in the arts of war. But in the end, this complaint represented the last cry of a dying breed of samurai aristocrats who were losing their place to the 'low'.

Heroic virtues were in short supply in the 40 years that followed, as the other great unifiers Toyotomi Hideyoshi (1536–98) and Tokugawa Ieyasu (1542–1616) succeeded Nobunaga.

Hideyoshi, a one-time sandal-bearer, murdered several members of his family to ensure his son's accession, and Ieyasu trained his cannon on female residents during a siege of his enemy's castle. Perhaps surprisingly, then, it was during Ieyasu's reign that the principles of bushidō were codified for the first time. At the beginning of the seventeenth century, Ieyasu had decreed there

Above: A fantasy scene showing 'the last samurai' Saigō Takamori committing seppuku as American gunboats approach. In reality, Takamori died on dry land at the Battle of Shiroyama.

Facing page: Two rōnin battle it out in the snow. Rōnin were masterless samurai or 'wave men'; destined to wander aimlessly like the waves in the sea.

would be 'no more wars' and by 1615 he had ensured that this would be a reality. The subsequent Edo Period brought 250 years of peace, and the emergence of many bushidō texts on how a warrior ought to behave outside of the theatre of conflict.

Life in the Edo Period became increasingly strained for the samurai, who were now a closed caste at the top of a social order that included peasants, artisans and merchants. Samurai were legally allowed to behead anyone who did not show them the proper respect, but they found themselves trapped within their own feudal system. The warriors were paid a rice stipend to stand battle-ready at their daimyō's castle residence, but this barely covered their costs. Other samurai were made unemployed. These rōnin, or masterless samurai, were then left to drift aimlessly around Japan.

Often rōnin got into trouble brawling and making a nuisance of themselves in provincial towns. Soon a law was passed that if two samurai were involved in a violent dispute both would be accountable, regardless of who was actually to blame. The punishment for this, alongside other crimes such as harbouring Christians and striking a superior, was the same: seppuku.

Seppuku, often known more coarsely as hara-kiri in the West, is considered one of the most painful possible ways to die. The bravest samurai were those who made the longest open cut and let their viscera hang from the wound. As such, a samurai about to perform seppuku was allowed to have a second waiting nearby to behead him at

the crucial moment and end his suffering. Seppuku manuals suggested leaving a flap of skin on the samurai's neck to prevent his head rolling away or hitting an official.

With the deterrent of seppuku to keep bored samurai in check, it was suggested they spend their time on more cultural pursuits such as tea ceremonies and calligraphy. In reality, many samurai struggled to survive and were forced to take up part-time jobs trading bamboo or making umbrellas. Some even sold their swords, or replaced the blade with bamboo to keep up appearances.

By the nineteenth century, the samurais' position in the martial order of Japan became increasingly difficult to justify. Ironically, their role as protectors of the country would be called upon in the mid-nineteenth century, over 200 years after the Shōgun closed Japan's borders to foreigners. It caused great consternation when, in 1853, four American warships steamed into Edo Bay and demanded that Japan reopen her doors. After the period of isolation, to Japanese eyes the modern warships were futuristic vessels that instantly rendered samurai weapons useless. All the Shōgun could do was throw up canvas forts with painted cannons, unaware that the Americans could watch the deception through another modern technology: binoculars.

End of an Era
The Shōgun's inability to subdue these new barbarians sealed his fate and consequently that of the samurai. After the samurai staged a coup to reinstate the Emperor as the true ruler of Japan, the Emperor himself abolished the samurai. But while the samurai had spent centuries slowly expiring, a last warrior staged a final bid for power. In 1877 Saigō Takamori went up against a new national army carrying breech-loading rifles, and went down with his sword held high, like the samurai of old.

In the end Takamori and the caste known as the samurai became the victims of the successes of their golden period. After Nobunaga, Hideyoshi and Ieyasu had fought so hard to end centuries of civil war and unite the country that there was little left for them to do. However, it is the story of how they achieved this peace that gives the golden age of the samurai such an enduring appeal.

Above: Saigō Takamori's grave in Nanshu Cemetery, Kagoshima. Takamori's last charge against modern weaponry from the West spelled the end for the samurai.

Facing page: Great emphasis was placed on the importance of tea ceremonies during Japan's Edo Period. With no wars to fight, warriors were encouraged into more cultural pursuits.

The Unification of Japan

Japan's so called 'golden period', which unified its provinces and led to 200 years of peace under the Tokugawa regime, followed centuries of violence and civil war that left the country divided and leaderless.

The trouble began in the mid-fifteenth century, when Ashikaga Yorimasa – a weak and decadent Shōgun – all but renounced his post, opening the way to the strongest contender. Those who sought power were the daimyō, warlords who ruled over the clans and provinces of Japan. Their fight to unite the country under one central ruler would see Japan splinter further into warring regional factions. This eventually led to a fundamental shift in the country's political model, as those with the greatest military might won out over those born with an aristocratic title. The movement even had a name: 'gekokujō', or 'the low overcomes the high'. This meant, for the first time in samurai history, that the low-born man could fight his way to the top using his brains and brawn alone. Those who achieved this goal did so with alarming speed and brutality. Among them are the three characters central to Japan's history: Oda Nobunaga (1534–82), Toyotomi Hideyoshi (1536–98) and Tokugawa Ieyasu (1542–1616). Of these, Hideyoshi, the one-time sandal-bearer and foot soldier who united the provinces, best represents the gekokujō ideal.

Gekokujō was only made possible by the slow decline of the Ashikaga Shōgunate, which ruled from the imperial capital of Kyōto. The Ashikaga had been pivotal in ending a period of war and confusion when two Emperors – one in the north and one in the south – ruled Japan at the same time. Although the Emperor was supposedly picked according to a mandate from heaven, the regional

Facing page: Shōgun Ashikaga Yoshimitsu's famous Golden Pavilion was equalled only by his Palace of Flowers, which was twice the size of the Emperor's palace.

Right: The Ashikaga Shōgunate reached its zenith under Yoshimitsu, who solved the country's two-emperor system. After Yoshimitsu, the Ashikaga fell into a slow decline.

samurai clans found they had to swear allegiance to one of the two. An era of regional clashes predictably followed, as both Emperors vied for control. Clans learned to change sides whenever it suited their needs. Sometimes neighbouring clans staged mock battles in which no blood was actually spilt, while their mock reports recounted 'great enemy numbers' and 'heroic fighting on either side'.

Peasant Revolt

As the country descended into regional conflict, the biggest losers were the 'low' – the peasants. Instead of dealing with one imperial official or tax collector, the peasantry often had to suffer two, one from each Emperor. Their anger soon erupted into protests and revolts. But in 1392, a cunning Ashikaga Shōgun called Yoshimitsu settled the two-Emperor issue by ordering a system of alternate rule. In reality the southern Emperor never got a turn, which suited Yoshimitsu who enjoyed a relationship of mutual admiration with the northern Emperor in Kyōto. Yoshimitsu cut a curious figure as Shōgun. He improved trade with China, built the 'Temple of the Golden Pavilion' and supported the arts and cultural traditions such as tea ceremonies. He also did what a Shōgun should – his shugo military governors largely kept the peace in the provinces and collected revenue for the imperial coffers.

But not all of Yoshimitsu's successors were made of the same stuff. If Yoshimitsu represented the high-water mark of the Ashikaga clan, his descendants only left a grimy ring. The worst of all was Yorimasa, who became Shōgun in 1443 at seven years of age. From the start, Yorimasa was a reluctant and uninterested ruler who collected taxes only to indulge himself in various artistic pursuits. It would have been of little concern to Yorimasa that under his watch, provincial clans were building strong and powerful armies, and becoming almost completely independent from Shōgunal control.

Under Yorimasa, it was only a matter of time before a serious conflict broke out between two or more vying clans. It was of course the Shōgun's role to keep the peace and prevent provincial struggles, but instead Yorimasa pawned off his armour to pay his entertainment bill. The Shōgunal hold on Japan was soon to slip completely from the Ashikaga grasp.

Sengoku Period (1467–1615)

Considering the increasingly ineffectual rule of the Ashikaga, it is perhaps fitting that the Sengoku Jidai, or 'the Age of the Country at War', began with a dispute over a succession claim to the Ashikaga Shōgunate. As the dispute boiled over, samurai from the two houses at its heart, the Hosokawa and the Yamana, met each other to wage war in the capital itself. Citizens of Kyōto fled the city as samurai took over homes, dug trenches across streets and began a series of raids on enemy dwellings. The conflict, known as the Ōnin War, lasted 11 years and reduced Kyōto to a pile of blackened, burning rubble. By the end, the samurai

Above: Hosokawa Katsumoto battled against the Yamana clan in the inconclusive Ōnin War. Kyōto was razed to the ground during the conflict.

Facing page: Shōgun Ashikaga Yorimasa was more interested in indulging himself than maintaining order. His Silver Pavilion, an imitation of his grandfather's Golden Pavilion, was never completed.

themselves moved away from the former front lines of the city centre and gangs of robbers, looters and other opportunists moved in. It was said that Ashikaga Yorimasa held poetry readings and tea ceremonies as the city fell around him.

But even after the fighting in Kyōto had played itself out, the disease of warfare had spread to the city's outlying districts and into the provinces. Now, the provincial samurai clans, who had been quietly power-building for nearly 200 years, were seizing the chance to use their military training. At the head of each clan was the daimyō, whose main aim was to hold control of his domain and conquer the jurisdictions of others. The final prize was, of course, the Shōgunate itself and the chance to rule over all of Japan. During this period, some samurai clans were simply wiped out while other smaller factions were obliged to join forces to stay alive.

The nature of warfare itself changed in the Sengoku Jidai. Romantic notions of mounted duels and battlefield decorum became as rare as aristocratic samurai leaders. Marching into replace them were the common foot soldiers, the ashigaru, armed with matchlock arquebuses.

The ashigaru would become the mainstay of samurai clan armies, and clever daimyō would go to great lengths to keep them happy. They depended on both the produce from peasant fields in peacetime and their presence on the battlefield during periods of war. Disaffected ashigaru could

and did show their displeasure by leaving to fight for a neighbouring daimyō. Other unhappy commoners could join a union called the ikki. The protesting peasants of the ikki first marched against the rice merchants and moneylenders who had grown rich from their labour. Groups of ikki who followed a sect of Buddhism called Jōdo Shinshū, or the 'True Pure Land', were known as Ikkō-ikki. The Ikkō-ikki became the first commoners to overthrow the samurai clan of the Kaga province and rule in their place. These Ikkō-ikki, upholding the ethos of gekokujō, would prove to be a military force equal to those of the mightiest samurai daimyō in the years to come.

Financial Problems of the Elite

At the other end of the social scale, things could not be worse. As the samurai clans fought for supremacy in the provinces, the lives of the Emperors and Shōguns in the capital were difficult. The Emperor simply had no money. The revenue from 250 landholdings across Japan before the Sengoku Jidai had shrunk to only 34 landholdings during the Warring States era. As such, ceremonies became modest and seldom-held affairs, the palace gardens grew unkempt and some of the emperors had to sell their private art collections. When Emperor Go-Tsuchimikado died in 1501, there was no money to bury him, and his successor was only able to hold his coronation with a cash gift from the Ikkō-ikki. The finances of the Shōgunate were no better, and the Shōgun, like the Emperor, became a mere figurehead.

Above: Uesugi Kenshin was a distinguished daimyō whose gentlemanly methods of combat would become completely outdated during the Sengoku Jidai.

Waging Gentlemanly War

Two of the early Sengoku Jidai's most colourful daimyō were Takeda Shingen and Uesugi Kenshin. They represented the last of the gentlemen warriors, who conducted their warfare according to the honourable traditions of old. Every year for five years in a row the armies of Kenshin and Shingen met in the same place on the plain of Kawanakajima to do battle. Sometimes, when one army had gained the upper hand it would withdraw as a sign of respect for the opposition. When Shingen's salt supply was cut off by Kenshin's ally, the Hōjō clan, Kenshin sent Shingen a supply of salt from his own stock, commenting that he 'fought with swords, not salt.'

Right: The Battle of Kawanakajima was an annual event fought between Uesugi Kenshin and Takeda Shingen. Both daimyō would ensure the battle ended in a draw.

Right: Oda Nobunaga was a brilliant and ruthless general who put thousands of innocents to the sword during the unification of Japan.

By the mid 1500s Japan had become chaotic and consumed by an endless series of regional battles. There was no central power. It was only a matter of time before a warring daimyō would judge himself strong enough to march on Kyōto and seize control.

ODA NOBUNAGA

It is characteristic of the gekokujō tradition of the age that the first great unifier of Japan was a ruthlessly ambitious upstart with no aristocratic pretentions. Oda Nobunaga was the son of a Owari province landowner who had inherited his father's lands as a 17-year-old in 1551. The endowment caused an immediate rift between his family members but this mattered little to Nobunaga, who had a reputation for mulish and unruly behaviour. He is reported to have acted so badly at his father's funeral that an Oda retainer felt compelled to commit seppuku to rebuke him. This action seemed to focus Nobunaga's ambitions, as the teenager set about conquering the splintered factions that made up Owari and unified the province under his rule as daimyō.

Nobunaga's ascent to power was rapid and relentless, his methods cunning, efficient and brutal. But he was not the only regional daimyō with aspirations. In fact, compared with the mighty samurai houses of the mid-sixteenth century – Hōjō, Takeda, Uesugi and Imagawa – the Oda clan was a mere minnow among piranhas. Of these rivals,

Nobunaga's greatest foe was Imagawa Yoshimoto. In 1554, he was a cultivated 35-year-old daimyō at the peak of his career. The Imagawa could trace its lineage back to the mighty Taira clan, and Yoshimoto was directly related to heroes of the Gempei War. Under his control were the Mikawa, Totomi and Suruga provinces, which, as fate would have it, lay directly next to the Oda province of Owari. Yoshimoto planned to invade Owari, but this was not his main goal. He intended to march on Kyōto itself and become the first regional daimyō to seize the coveted although largely empty title of Shōgun.

By 1558, Yoshimoto had started attacking Nobunaga's fortresses along the border. In charge of these frontier skirmishes was one of Yoshimoto's rising stars – a 17-year-old samurai called Tokugawa Ieyasu. Ieyasu was to be the last of the great unifiers of Japan. His reign followed that of Nobunaga and Toyotomi Hideyoshi, a young samurai who was also involved in the conflict between the Imagawa and the Oda. But unlike Ieyasu, Hideyoshi was fighting on the side of Nobunaga. Here, his guile and unflinching loyalty had led to a rapid rise through the ranks unmatched by any other samurai. Hideyoshi's ascent also represents the pinnacle of gekokujō achievement. He was born the son of a simple Owari peasant, whose main ambition for his son was to join the priesthood. Instead, Hideyoshi absconded from the monastery and became a foot

Left: Oda Nobunaga was a formidable opponent in battle, but it was not until he adopted the arquebus that his army became an unstoppable force.

Right: The sixteenth century clan domains of Japan. Those clans that bordered a powerful and ambitious neighbour had good cause to worry during the Sengoku Jidai.

soldier in the Owari army. After stealing money to buy armour, Hideyoshi managed to join those fighting directly under Nobunaga. He was, for a time, the daimyō's sandal-bearer. Hideyoshi's fearlessness and cunning in battle soon caught Nobunaga's eye, and in short time he became one of the daimyō's leading generals.

Dawn Assault

Hideyoshi would play a big role in defending the Owari province against Imagawa Yoshimoto's army, as the daimyō tried to push through to Kyōto. Owari was the first of three provinces that Yoshimoto would need to cross to reach the capital, and, with a 40,000-strong samurai army it is unlikely he considered Nobunaga a serious threat. The events began on a summer's day in June 1560, when news reached Nobunaga at his Kiyosu Castle that one of his outlying fortresses had been overrun. The Imagawa attack, led by Tokugawa Ieyasu, had come at dawn and relied heavily on arquebus fire. Only hours later reports indicated that a second fortress had fallen. The sheer numbers of the enemy force, combined with the ferocity of the fighting, suggested an all-out invasion rather than another traditional skirmish on the province's periphery.

There were two options open to Nobunaga. He could wait at Kiyosu and for the inevitable siege, or go on the offensive and attack the Imagawa. To the

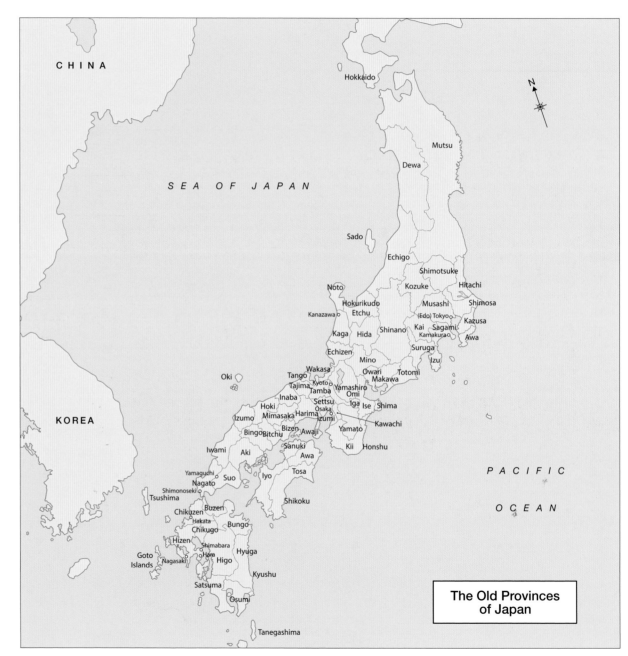

The Old Provinces of Japan

The Battle of Okehazama

As Nobunaga approached Okehazama he sent scouts ahead. In his army's camp in a forested gorge, Imagawa Yoshimoto was enjoying the traditional ritual of viewing the heads of enemies taken from the Oda fortresses. Each head had a label giving the samurai's name as well as the name of the warrior who had killed him. So far the victories against the Oda had been well-won and Yoshimoto was pleased. A mood of celebration reigned at the Imagawa camp; after several hours of sake consumption there was something of a carnival atmosphere. Meanwhile, Nobunaga led his troops to a nearby hill where they built a decoy camp, complete with banners and flags. The intention was to keep the Imagawa's eye distracted while the Oda planned a surprise attack.

It was a hot and sticky day in Owari, and in the early afternoon a thunderstorm broke. The subsequent downpour provided the perfect cover for Nobunaga and his men who approached the Imagawa camp with stealth and speed. As the rain lifted, the Oda samurai charged at the Imagawa, who were so shocked and unprepared that many simply ran for the hills. Yoshimoto himself was napping in his tent when he was roused by the commotion outside. Thinking it was the sound of his own men's revelries, Yoshimoto stormed from his tent to call for quiet. As he did so, he met an Oda samurai rushing at him with a spear. As he fumbled for his sword, another Oda retainer beheaded Yoshimoto. Now leaderless, the Imagawa force melted away, leaving dozens of fallen samurai behind.

Above: The grave of Imagawa Yoshimoto. Imagawa Yoshimoto was the first daimyō to underestimate Oda Nobunaga, his young neighbour. The 1560 Battle of Okehazama would be Yoshimoto's undoing.

24

Left: Arquebusiers would sometimes cover their matchlock mechanism with a lacquered box so they could fire in the rain.

shock and amazement of his military commanders, Nobunaga chose the latter. An offensive seemed suicidal – Nobunaga commanded an army of only 2000 samurai, which meant the Imagawa outnumbered him by twenty to one. Nevertheless, the extreme odds did not seem to dampen the daimyō's mood, and he hummed merrily to himself as he led his army towards the Imagawa force encamped in a gorge near the small village of Okehazama.

The Battle of Okehazama lasted only a matter of minutes, but it was a pivotal point in Nobunaga's rise to power. It also allied him with Tokugawa Ieyasu – who defected to Nobunaga alongside hundreds of other defeated Imagawa warriors – and brought his name to the attention of the Emperor. The victory at Okehazama represented gekokujō at its purest and most practical. Nobunaga, a simple landowner's son, had defeated the army of an experienced, aristocratic daimyō at the head of a vastly superior force.

Nobunaga had shown that being without the necessary pedigree was no obstacle to success. Naked ambition, strategic cunning and complete ruthlessness could now win the day. The tradition of mounted duels between gentlemen warriors was over. Now, a large army of ashigaru foot soldiers carrying arquebuses would determine success in war – and the strategic use of arquebuses on the battlefield was Nobunaga's specialty.

Right: The sword, bow and naginata were the traditional weapons of the samurai. Here, they are styled by Minamoto Yoshitsune and the warrior monk Benkei.

The Tanegashima

The use of firearms was unknown in a warrior nation centred on the sword. In fact the samurai's introduction to this revolutionary weapon came about by accident. In 1543 a fleet of Portuguese merchants were caught in a storm and washed up on the rocky Japanese island of Tanegashima, south of Kyūshū.

The shipwreck would have been unremarkable if not for the arquebuses the sailors were carrying. The samurai had experienced gunpowder before – Mongol invaders had put it to deadly use when attacking Japan in the thirteenth century. But the power of gunpowder harnessed in a small, portable weapon was something new and of great interest to the local Tanegashima daimyō. After lessons in the gun's manufacture, Tanegashima swordsmiths set about producing large quantities of arquebuses, thereafter commonly known in Japan as 'the tanegashima'.

The introduction of the arquebus onto the battlefield was controversial. To veteran samurai warriors, the weapon seemed to contravene every rule of warfare by which they had lived and died. After all, they had spent their entire lives perfecting the art of battle and training for an honourable death by the sword. But now they could be brought down by a weapon that an ashigaru could be trained to use in a single day.

The arquebus meant the lowest-ranking member of a samurai army could use the weapon to kill a high-ranking warrior who until recently could often trace his lineage to the original aristocratic samurai of Japan. But this was the new way of war. Armies would still be led by mounted samurai leaders, but the use of bows and arrows would be slowly replaced by guns, stockades and formidable stone fortresses. The young daimyō leading the way in all of these innovations of war was Oda Nobunaga.

Nobunaga realized the importance of the arquebus in battle. He did not use the weapon just to supplement his back line of archers, as the older daimyō Takeda Shingen had done. Instead, Nobunaga used the guns upfront, in rotating lines of ashigaru shielded from an enemy assault by a fence or stockade. The weapon led to great carnage on the battlefield and ensured the strength of Nobunaga's army. To ensure a constant supply line of guns, gunpowder and ammunition, Nobunaga began seizing ports that traded with foreign countries and towns containing silver mines. Now that he had the weaponry, Nobunaga's campaign for power began in earnest. The ideology of his long march to Kyōto and the unification of Japan's regional clans was simple – take what you need, join with willing clans and eliminate any that stand in your way.

Courted by the Court

Nobunaga's policy of conquest and control acquired a certain legitimacy when Emperor Ōgimachi wrote a letter referring to him as the 'famous general with no peer in any age'. After the flattery came a request for a favour, as Ōgimachi asked Nobunaga to recover the imperial holdings in Owari and also his recently conquered territory of Mino. Ōgimachi also wondered if Nobunaga could help out financially with repairs on the imperial palace. There were further requests for help, this time from Ashikaga Yoshiaki, brother of the murdered Shōgun and rightful heir to the title. Yoshiaki had appealed for help in the past from any daimyō that he considered had the strength of arms to support him. In the end it was Nobunaga who heeded Yoshiaki's call. Nobunaga was not of aristocratic blood and so could not become Shōgun. But he could certainly become the power behind one, and the Ashikaga had had many years of practice as Shōgunal puppets.

In 1568, Nobunaga plucked Yoshiaki from his hideaway in the province of Echizen and marched with him at the head of a large army towards Kyōto. On the way he conquered parts of Ise, Iga and Ōmi. The reigning Shōgun and the Matsunaga clan pulling his strings fled Kyōto as soon as Nobunaga approached. Yoshiaki was quickly made the fifteenth and last Ashikaga Shōgun. At the beginning there were promising signs for Yoshiaki, whose main aim was to restore the Shōgunate to its true glory. From the outset he acted like the man in charge: he sued daimyōs for peace and attempted to recover imperial landholdings and estates. It also appeared that Nobunaga was supporting Yoshiaki's position. He built the Shōgun a large and lavish castle in Kyōto that boasted moats, bridges, stone towers and ostentatious interior fittings. But trouble was coming. Yoshiaki was sent 16 statutes by Nobunaga, one of which stated that the Shōgun must adopt without question any policy put forward by Nobunaga. Access to the Shōgun was also to be restricted. Warriors, daimyōs and leaders from religious sects would be forbidden an audience with Yoshiaki.

Things went on in this manner until in 1570 Nobunaga heard that Yoshiaki was plotting a revolt. Nobunaga turned the screw with another set of Shōgunal orders. One of the new statutes read: 'Since the affairs of the realm have in fact been put in Nobunaga's hands, Nobunaga may take measures against anyone whatsoever according to his own discretion and without the need to obtain the Shōgun's agreement.' In other words, Nobunaga was now free to do whatever he liked, to whomever, whenever he pleased. The gloves were off and Nobunaga's ambition stood plain. Between 1570 and 1573 Nobunaga went to war with six samurai houses: the Askura, Asai, Takeda, Rokkaku, Miyoshi and Matsunga.

Leading his numerous campaigns during this time were his two greatest generals – Hideyoshi and Ieyasu. But despite their brilliance, Nobunaga was fighting on several different fronts and his army was stretched. One recurring thorn in Nobunaga's side was the Ikkō-ikki, who had built temples and fortresses in Owari, Kaga, Echizen and other strategic locations in the provinces surrounding Kyōto. The Ikkō-ikki were a threat through their political and economic influence as well as their military clout. They had allied themselves with almost all of Nobunaga's enemies and there was an Ikkō-ikki stronghold near every major trade route. One of the Ikkō-ikki allies was a much older order of warrior-monks – the Enryaku-ji sōhei from Mount Hiei. The Enryaku-ji had a well-established history of agitation and rebellion against ruling factions, including the Oda.

Indiscriminate Slaughter

Now, Nobunaga decided to make an example of them. In 1571, 30,000 of Nobunaga's samurai marched on the monastery at Mount Hiei in what was to become one of his most brutal and infamous acts. In the dead of night, the warriors encircled the monastery and at dawn 'entered the fortress and put all to the fire and sword', recorded Portuguese missionary Luis Frois. This was wholesale butchery, with men, women and children beheaded where they stood or lay. Nobunaga's men made sure none hid or escaped and afterwards set fire to the entire monastery, burning down over 2000 buildings.

Back in Kyōto, Ashikaga Yoshiaki had found a sympathetic daimyō to champion his cause against the oppressor Oda Nobunaga. Takeda Shingen was a onetime ally of Nobunaga's who now broke the terms of their union and made ready to march a formidable army of 20,000 samurai on Kyōto. But standing between Shingen and his quarry was Hamamatsu Castle, the headquarters of Tokugawa Ieyasu. Shingen's troops outnumbered Ieyasu's by

Above: The Battle of Mikatagahara pitted one-time Nobunaga ally Takeda Shingen against the formidable Tokugawa Ieyasu. Ieyasu ended up fleeing the battleground on horseback.

Facing page: The Battle of Mikatagahara proved that a cavalry charge could outdo a firing line of arquebusiers. Here, a similar charge is staged in Kurosawa's film *Ran*.

three to one, but buoyed by 3000 reinforcements from Nobunaga and his own unshakable self-belief, Ieyasu decided to meet Shingen on the plain of Mikatagahara for a pitched battle. So it was that on the afternoon of 25 January 1573, as the snow began to fall, two facing lines of warriors came together like the samurai armies of old. Shingen organized his forward line into a 'fish scale' formation, while Ieyasu opted for that of a 'stork's wing', which maximized the use of arquebus fire along his front line. While the arquebus is largely considered the battlefield game-changer of sixteenth century Japanese warfare, it would be outdone at Mikatagahara by an old-fashioned samurai cavalry charge. The arquebus ashigaru at the centre of Ieyasu's front line were completely overrun by the

horsemen, while his flanks only just managed to hold themselves in a 'wing' formation.

A second charge, this time led by Takeda Katsuyori, threw Ieyasu's army into disarray, forcing Ieyasu himself to flee. As Ieyasu rode back to the safety of Hamamatsu Castle, rumours quickly circulated that the day was lost. The castle's inhabitants began preparing to strengthen the walls for the inevitable Takeda siege. But Ieyasu ordered the gates to be kept open and the torches lit inside to guide back his retreating army. Ieyasu's tactic, known as the 'empty fort strategy', bewildered the Takeda army as it approached the castle and made Shingen suspect a trap. Instead of attacking the castle, which would have been easily overrun, the Takeda stopped and pitched camp for the night a short distance from its walls.

Some accounts report that during the night, the Takeda camp was infiltrated by Oda ninjas (mercenaries), who killed some prominent samurai and threw the camp into confusion. Other accounts say that Shingen was brought news of an imminent force made up of Nobunaga and Uesugi Kenshin samurai that far outnumbered his own. Whatever the reason, something persuaded Shingen to call off his attack on Hamamatsu Castle and retreat. Takeda Shingen would have one attempt at an all-out attack on Kyōto, this time at the front of an army made up of Takeda, Asai, Asakura and Ikkō-ikki warriors. He would get no further than Tokugawa Ieyasu's Noda Castle. Here, as the Takeda laid siege to the fortress, a lucky arquebus shot from an ashigaru killed Shingen as he approached the castle walls.

Nobunaga Strikes Back

The news of Shingen's death was music to Nobunaga's ears and gave him the impetus to move against his more local rivals. First he surrounded Kyōto and demanded a large tribute from the nobles and merchants of the city. When they refused he set fire to their homes. Next he marched a small samurai force to Ashikaga Yoshiaki's retreat near the Uji River and forced him into exile. Retribution against the Ikkō-ikki was next on Nobunaga's list and he set about attacking every one of their fortresses. Many of these assaults turned into sieges that lasted for several years before the strongholds were overcome. One example was the fortress of Nagashima located in a swampy delta between the Owari and Isa provinces. Nobunaga attacked the stronghold in three different sieges using heavy artillery fire from ships.

The final siege ended in 1574, when Nobunaga built a wooden palisade around Nagashima and set it alight. Not one of the 20,000 people living at Nagashima escaped the flames. Perhaps Nobunaga's best-known victory was against the Takeda clan in 1575, in a place called Nagashino. The battle, which ended in complete rout of the Takeda, is examined in more detail in Chapter 2. Nagashino cemented the place of the arquebus in samurai warfare and created the need for stronger stone fortresses to withstand sieges by gunpowder weapons.

Facing page: Takeda Shingen's grave in Kofu, Yamanashi Prefecture. Shingen's death provoked different responses in his rivals: Oda Nobunaga was overjoyed, while Uesugi Kenshin wept.

Right: A memorial stone at the ruins of Oda Nobunaga's Azuchi Castle. Azuchi would be burned to the ground by Nobunaga's murderer, Akechi Mitsuhide.

Nobunaga seems to have had these new fortifications in mind when he started building Azuchi Castle in 1576. The name of his castle, in combination with Hideyoshi's Momoyama Castle, lends the era its name: the Azuchi-Momoyama Period, which would last until 1600. Azuchi Castle was built outside Kyōto, but close enough to monitor the city's activities. Azuchi was a statement – a stone symbol of Nobunaga's power and his ambition for a permanent position at the top. Its walls were thick and high, punctured with loopholes for arqebuses to fire through, and its keep was impregnable. It was a castle fit for a conquering warlord, and it dominated the landscape.

By 1581, Nobunaga was nearing his goal of unifying all of the samurai clans under his rule, but some rivals remained. The most powerful were the Mori, whom Nobunaga's general Akechi Mitsuhide had unsuccessfully tried to bring to heel. Mitsuhide's poor efforts would see him replaced by Toyomoti Hideyoshi, and would contribute to his later hatred for Nobunaga. Hideyoshi had moments of brilliance against the Mori, including his siege of the clan's Takamatsu Castle in 1582.

The castle was built on low-lying land, and Hideyoshi cleverly diverted the water from two nearby rivers to flood the defenders out. The effect was to create a lake around Takamatsu and a rising

The Death of Nobunaga

The events at Honnōji were recounted by Portuguese missionary Luis Frois, who was in Kyōto at the time of Nobunaga's death.

'We at once began to hear musket shots and see flames. After this, another report came and we learned that it had not been a brawl but that Akechi had turned traitor and enemy of Nobunaga and had him surrounded. When Akechi's men reached the palace gates, they at once entered as nobody was there to resist them because there had been no suspicion of their treachery. Nobunaga had just washed his hands and face and was drying himself with a towel when they found him and forthwith shot him in the side with an arrow. Pulling the arrow out, he came out carrying a naginata, a weapon with a long blade made after the fashion of a scythe. He fought for some time, but after receiving a shot in the arm he retreated into his chamber and shut the doors. Some say that he cut his belly, while others believe that he set fire to the palace and perished in the flames. What we do know, however, is that of this man, who made everyone tremble not only at the sound of his voice but even at the mention of his name, there did not remain even a small hair which was not reduced to dust and ashes.'

Right: Luis Frois was a Portuguese missionary and friend of Oda Nobunaga's. He was staying in Kyōto at the time of the daimyō's assassination.

Left: Arquebusiers fire a volley during a Tokyo parade of the Teppo Hyakunincho, or '100 sharpshooters of the Edo Period'.

tide that brought snakes and rats into the castle. But Mori reinforcements were on the way, and Hideyoshi sent word to Nobunaga that he needed more men. Nobunaga dispatched every available samurai, including most of his own 2000-strong bodyguard. He then made his way to the Honnōji monastery in Kyōto. Among those coming to Hideyoshi's aid was Akechi Mitsuhide and a large force of samurai retainers. The army did not get far. Popular accounts say Akechi Mitsuhide stopped at a fork in the road, muttering that 'the enemy is in the Honnōji', and turning his troops back towards Kyōto.

There are many theories why Mitsuhide hated Nobunaga. Some say it was because he had been disgraced when Nobunaga replaced him with Hideyoshi to fight the Mori. Other accounts say Nobunaga overruled Mitsuhide's order to execute prisoners who in turn took their revenge by murdering members of Mitsuhide's family. Another story has Nobunaga humiliating Mitsuhide by grabbing him around the neck and using his head as a drum. Whatever the reason, Mitsuhide was about to take his vengeance as his warriors surrounded Honnōji and assassinated Nobunaga.

It is ironic that Nobunaga was brought down by a weapon for which he had rewritten the samurai rulebook. The efficient use of the arquebus in battle was his legacy. He replaced the mounted bow-and-arrow-wielding samurai with lines of ashigaru

Right: One of many statues of Toyotomi Hideyoshi, the second of the three great samurai unifiers who was known to Oda Nobunaga as 'Little Monkey'.

carrying arquebuses. And with these weapons he mowed down thousands of samurai warriors who been raised on stories of heroism and bravery from the Gempei War. As a general, Nobunaga was brutal and merciless. After his battles, Nobunaga would order that fugitives be hunted down and killed 'yama yama, tani tani' ('on every hill, in every valley'). Men, women and children were burned to death indiscriminately in his sieges at Mount Hiei and Nagashima. But Nobunaga's reign could also be seen as a necessary evil on the path to unification. For the next great ruler would not unite only by conquest and putting enemy clans to the sword, but also through conciliation.

TOYOTOMI HIDEYOSHI

Toyotomi Hideyoshi found himself in a difficult position when the news reached him of Nobunaga's death. He was, of course, trying to force his enemies from their castle at Takamatsu, but also expecting enemy reinforcements at any time. Nobunaga's other great general, Tokugawa Ieyasu, was detained in Sakai. Akechi Mitsuhide had been cunning in his timing. The assassination took place when every Oda army was far from Kyōto, fighting clans still hostile to Nobunaga's rule. It would take time for them to launch a retaliatory

strike. It was also unclear whether this was their best course of action. Most samurai clans met the news of Nobunaga's death with trepidation and bewilderment. Many were pleased that Nobunaga was gone, but where did it leave them? After plundering and burning Azuchi Castle, Mitsuhide began to behave like Nobunaga's successor. He sent expensive gifts to the Emperor and the temples, and granted Kyōto citizens a reduction in taxes. As a result the imperial court felt obliged to cautiously congratulate Mitsuhide. Curiously, Nobunaga's son, his generals and clans allied to the Oda did not launch an immediate attack, although Ieyasu began massing troops. Instead, daimyō friendly to Nobunaga hesitated. All, that is, except one.

Peace Negotiations

Hideyoshi was a brilliant negotiator and rather than try to defeat the Mori or leave his war with them half-won he decided to cut them a deal. The Mori, all but destroyed anyway, gladly accepted Hideyoshi's terms of peace. Hideyoshi was then free to march on Kyōto, picking up numbers of samurai from friendly clans along the way. So it was that 13 days after Nobunaga's death Hideyoshi met the pretender Akechi Mitsuhide with his vastly inferior army at Yamazaki near Kyōto. Of the battle there is little to tell. Mitsuhide's force was swiftly and decisively overrun and the general himself forced to flee into nearby rice fields. Here, Mitsuhide was set upon by local robbers who plundered and killed him. He would be remembered afterwards as 'The 13-Day Shōgun'.

Right: Akechi Mitsuhide suffered something of an ignominious end: he was chased into a rice field and murdered by robbers.

The rout at Yamazaki left Hideyoshi in charge. He had wasted no time in avenging Nobunaga's death and now looked like becoming Nobunaga's successor. And why not? The man Nobunaga called 'little monkey' after his shrunken physique was also called 'war-god' for his military prowess. Now Hideyoshi had justified his position as his master's loyal servant, even after death – a favourite theme among the samurai. Hideyoshi was also popular among his men. He was, after all, one of them. As the epitome of the gekokujō tradition, Hideyoshi had cast off his peasant's shackles and was now heading for the pinnacle of power.

Conference at Kiyosu

Not everyone liked the idea of having Hideyoshi as ruler. Nobunaga's sons, especially, resented being supplanted as heirs by the 'little monkey'. This would become apparent at a conference at Kiyosu Castle in Owari. The conference, which included Nobunaga's important generals and family members, was designed to deal with the tricky issue of succession and the division of Nobunaga's territory.

Nobunaga's sons, Nobukatsu and Nobutaka, quickly clashed and the talks stalled. In response, the cunningly diplomatic Hideyoshi went into an adjoining room and reentered holding Nobunaga's three-year-old grandson, Sambōshi. Making Sambōshi Nobunaga's heir was a shrewd move. The

Right: Akechi Mitsuhide suffered something of an ignominious end: he was chased into a rice field and murdered by robbers.

Above: Shibata Katsuie was a senior daimyō who could not tolerate Toyotomi Hideyoshi's rule. He would retain his honour in death, despite his disloyalty.

Facing page: Gifu Castle was the headquarters of Nobunaga's son Oda Nobutaka. Nobutaka would twice raise armies against Hideyoshi from Gifu.

child was no threat to his uncles, and Nobunaga's territories could be divided up among his former generals. Nobunaga's conquests could be kept under one united authority and the status quo retained. The question of actual succession had been sidestepped.

Not everyone was happy. Shibata Katsuie, the senior member of the conference, had gained the Oda territory of Ōmi as well as keeping his Echizen territory. This was perhaps not a large enough slice of pie, as the disgruntled Katsuie immediately formed a clandestine alliance with another conference malcontent, Oda Nobutaka. Hideyoshi, on the other hand, was given control alongside three other daimyōs, none of whom decided to take the offer up. It was plain to see that of all the territory carved up at the Kiyosu conference, Hideyoshi had gained most.

Hideyoshi quickly set about stamping his authority on Kyōto and built a castle nearby at Yamazaki, the site of his recent victory against Mitsuhide. The castle was close enough to keep watch on the capital, but not so close as to imply a position of rule. However, his progress irked Shibata Katsuie and Oda Nobutaka, who could see that Hideyoshi was plotting. Nobutaka was first to act by declaring war on Hideyoshi. By the extraordinarily bad timing of his declaration alone, Nobutaka revealed both his age and inexperience. This was because Katsuie was snowed in at his domain at Echizen – as he was every winter – and would therefore be of no help to the impetuous Nobutaka.

Hideyoshi, on the other hand, was able to act quickly and decisively. He marched his army into Nobutaka's Mino province and surrounded his headquarters at Gifu Castle. Nobutaka buckled at the sight of Hideyoshi's samurai veterans and begged for mercy. Hideyoshi, in turn, was lenient. It was a sign of how much Hideyoshi's style differed from Nobunaga's, who would have almost certainly have razed the castle with the rebels inside.

Next, Hiedyoshi moved to deal with Shibata Katsuie, who was desperately waiting for an early spring thaw so he could march his army through the snowy passes of Echizen. In anticipation, Hideyoshi had built 13 forts in northern Ōmi against the inevitable offensive. But for a while no attack came. Instead news arrived that Nobutaka was amassing a new army against Hideyoshi at Gifu Castle. Hideyoshi immediately marched a large force to quell this latest uprising, but at the cost of his security at Ōmi.

No sooner had Hideyoshi departed than a Katsuie ally, Sakuma Morimasa, attacked the forts. By the time the news reached Hideyoshi, who once again routed Nobutaka's force at Gifu Castle, several of his Ōmi forts had fallen. Hideyoshi had no choice but to wheel his troops around and ride hard to Ōmi. Popular legend has Hideyoshi and his men covering the 80km (50 miles) in an improbable five hours.

Samurai Retreat

The Battle of Shizugatake that followed is considered by many historians to be the most important of Hideyoshi's career. It would also be one

Right: Hideyoshi issues a rallying cry on his war trumpet at the Battle of Shizugatake. Shizugatake was arguably Hideyoshi's most important battle. It was also the shortest.

of the shortest. Perhaps taken by hubris, Sakuma Morimasa thought he could plant a defensive line against Hideyoshi and destroy his troops as Nobunaga had done at the Battle of Nagashino. But instead the two forces joined in a melee on the pine-covered hills around the Shizugatake fortress. Sakuma Morimasa's army splintered in defeat and its remaining samurai beat a hasty retreat towards Echizen. Hideyoshi followed and there was a series of desperate and bloody clashes as the Toyotomi chased the Sakuma into Echizen and right up to the walls of Katsuie's Kitanosho Castle.

Katsuie himself had had no part in the fighting, but when he saw the day was lost he showed his traditional samurai spirit, setting fire to his own keep and stabbing his family to death before committing seppuku alongside 80 of his retainers. His partner Nobutaka also took his life in the usual ritualistic way upon hearing of Katsuie's demise.

Hideyoshi's Rising Star
The Battle of Shizugatake was a decisive victory for Hideyoshi and signalled his determination to rule. He admitted this in a letter to one of his generals describing the scene at Kitanosho Castle: 'I saw that

Facing page: A monument marks the site of the 1583 Battle of Shizugatake. The battle was played out among the pine trees of the hillside forest.

if we should let Shibata get his breath, the thing would be long drawn-out. I thought to myself: "This is the time to decide who shall govern Japan." Those around Hideyoshi responded favourably. He was congratulated by the Tokugawa, Uesugi and Hōjō clans and given a minor court rank by the Emperor. Better still, he was brought the head of Akechi Mitsuhide, which he put on display next to the ruins of the Honnōji monastery. By the end of 1582 Hideyoshi knew he was in the ascendant. He ruled over 30 provinces and had no active enemies. It was unlikely that he considered any of his long-term allies to be a threat at this time, but if samurai history had taught him anything it was to expect trouble from unexpected quarters. And there was of course one Nobunaga son left to fight for what he considered was his birthright.

So it was that in 1583 Hideyoshi learned that Oda Nobukatsu joined with none other than Tokugawa Ieyasu against him. Ieyasu was of course Hideyoshi's former comrade and the other great general who had won so much for Oda Nobunaga. Ieyasu was a powerful adversary, and if there was one daimyō with the skills and strength to win against Hideyoshi it was probably him. Why he went to war against Hideyoshi was less clear. Perhaps he was irritated that Hideyoshi had been the first to pick up Nobunaga's reins.

While Ieyasu had hesitated following his master's death, Hideyoshi had marched decisively against Mitsuhide and seized control. Ieyasu had also been conspicuously absent at the Kiyosu conference, although the carving up of domains did not stop him becoming one of the most powerful daimyōs in the country.

However, if Ieyasu believed war against Hideyoshi under Oda Nobukatsu's banner would bring him to power he was going to be disappointed. The conflict was a sporadic series of clashes that lasted little more than eight months and ended in stalemate. Surprisingly then, the result was win-win for both daimyō: Hideyoshi won back a close and powerful ally; Ieyasu won formal recognition to control the five provinces he had conquered.

This was typical of Hideyoshi's policy of unification. In almost all cases, those daimyō who had warred with Hideyoshi were at least publicly forgiven and allowed to keep most of their territory. In return, Hideyoshi would take some land for himself and retain the right to call upon the defeated daimyō's forces whenever needed. Enabling defeated daimyō to remain strong was a calculated risk on Hideyoshi's part. There were now 12 main daimyōs in central Japan who ruled over large and powerful domains. A united majority could easily topple Hideyoshi. So why did it not happen? Because, more or less, everyone got what they wanted. Unlike Nobunaga, Hideyoshi did not launch a purge. When opposed he would conquer and then conciliate, but he was not interested in slaughtering everything in his path and then hunting fugitives down in the style of Nobunaga's 'yama yama, tani tani'. As a result, all of the major daimyōs of Japan would sign a declaration of their allegiance to Hideyoshi by the end of the decade.

This left Hideyoshi free to carry on with empire building. In 1584 he constructed a massive castle at Ōsaka and was made Kampaku, or Regent, by the Emperor. Hideyoshi asserted in a letter that: 'The government of Japan will be made superior to anything since Yoritomo.' As Hideyoshi's star rose so did his personal strength of arms. In his conflict against Ieyasu, Hideyoshi's samurai carried slightly fewer than 5000 arquebuses. Troop numbers were also becoming staggeringly large. When putting down a rebellion on the island of Shikoku, Hideyoshi sent a force of 90,000 samurai, the largest offensive yet launched in the Azuchi-Momoyama Period. Soon after, Hideyoshi would dispatch an even larger army against the Shimazu clan of Kyūshū.

Christian Conflict

Kyūshū is the large island below Honshū where arquebuses first appeared on Japanese shores via a Portuguese shipwreck. With the muskets had also come missionaries, who converted many of the citizens of Kyūshū. This caused an ongoing conflict between Christians and non-Christians, as Buddhist shrines were desecrated and forced conversions became commonplace. There was also a recurring power play between the island's leading daimyō – the Christian Ōtomo Sōrin and his enemy Shimazu Yoshihisa. In the end, Sōrin travelled to Honshu to

Facing page: A re-enactment of the 1590 Siege of Odawara. It ended in a famous victory for Toyotomi Hideyoshi, who finally rid himself of his Hōjō foe.

appeal directly to Hideyoshi for help. He brought with him a large supply of tea, a great favourite of Hideyoshi's. Hideyoshi liked Sōrin's proposal. To become the absolute ruler of Japan he would need to conquer Kyūshū; sorting out a local difficulty would give him the best possible excuse. His resolve was strengthened when Shimazu Yoshihisa replied to Hideyoshi's calls for peace by insulting the newly invested Kampaku in a letter. His exact words on Hideyoshi's appointment were that the Emperor 'must have made a hasty choice.'

Hideyoshi's southern campaign had little chance of failing. His enormous force of nearly 300,000 samurai overwhelmed Yoshihisa in a matter of months. The once-proud daimyō kept his promise to shave his head in defeat and become a Buddhist monk. Hideyoshi, on the other hand, returned to a hero's welcome in Ōsaka and a new imperial post as Chancellor. In 1590, Hideyoshi put down the last threat to his power – the mighty Hōjō clan – in the Siege of Odawara Castle. Hideyoshi had achieved the dream of unification and brought the warring states together under his Toyotomi banner. Now he would have to retain the power he had won.

The Edicts

Hideyoshi's next step in consolidating his control was to issue a series of edicts explaining how his rule would manifest itself in law. These social,

A Letter Home

The conflict in Kyūshū was a precursor for Hideyoshi's much greater campaign of conquest overseas. Hideyoshi announced his intentions in a letter to his wife following his victory in Kyūshū: 'I will tell Korea that they should come to Japan to greet the Emperor. If no one comes from Korea, I will inform them that I will conquer them next year. I shall take control over China during our lifetime.' Then, as if to counterbalance this grandiose statement, Hideyoshi signed off with a personal message of insecurity: 'During this campaign, more and more grey hairs have grown and I have not plucked them out… I know that you would not mind. But I hate this grey hair.'

Right: Toyotomi Hideyoshi weathers a supernatural thunderstorm as all around him descends into chaos. Hideyoshi had no doubt that he would reign supreme over Korea and China.

The Collection of Swords

1. Farmers of all provinces are strictly forbidden to have in their possession any swords, short swords, bows, spears, firearms or other types of weapons. If unnecessary implements of war are kept, the collection of annual rent may become more difficult, and without provocation uprisings can be fomented. Therefore, those who perpetrate improper acts against samurai who receive a grant of land must be brought to trial and punished. However, in that event, their wet and dry fields will remain unattended, and the samurai will lose their rights to the yields from the fields. Therefore, the heads of the provinces, samurai who receive a grant of land and deputies must collect all the weapons described above and submit them to Hideyoshi's government.

2. The swords and short swords collected in the above manner will not be wasted. They will be used as nails and bolts in the construction of the Great Image of Buddha. In this way, farmers will benefit not only in this life but also in the lives to come.

3. If farmers possess only agricultural implements and devote themselves exclusively to cultivating the fields, they and their descendants will prosper. This compassionate concern for the well-being of the farms is the reason for the issuance of this edict, and such a concern is the foundation for the peace and security of the country and the joy and happiness of all the people.

All the implements cited above shall be collected and submitted forthwith.

Vermillion seal of Hideyoshi
Sixteenth year of Tensho [1588],
seventh month, eighth day

economic and political reforms were designed to control a population moving from centuries of regional warfare into a period of peace under one central leader.

The first edict concerned the missionary presence in Kyūshū. For Hideyoshi and his predecessors their gekokujō rise through the ranks would have been unthinkable without the use of the Portuguese arquebuses. Christianity on the other hand had become a divisive presence. It was well known that in Kyūshū missionaries had been secretly arming their converts. So, in 1587, Hideyoshi issued an edict banning Christian missionaries from Kyūshū: 'Japan is the land of the Gods. Diffusion here from the Kirishitan Country of a pernicious doctrine is most undesirable.'

Hideyoshi's 'sword hunt' edict was probably his most infamous and influential. It aimed to change the social structure of Japan, disarming the peasantry and making it illegal for anyone other than the samurai to carry weapons. This was an extraordinary challenge to the peasants, who for centuries had bore arms on behalf of their lord and province. To some extent the peasant's role in war had blurred lines of class, but now there was to be a defined feudal social system, with the samurai at the top and everyone else below. Perhaps the most surprising thing about the edict is that it came from Hideyoshi, the former son of a peasant. But now that he had climbed to the top he was determined to prevent others from following.

Hideyoshi issued another edict making it illegal for samurai to re-enter village life or to be hired for any alternative work. It also prohibited farmers from leaving their fields and seeking any other employment. Finally, it made it not only unadvisable for anyone to hire a samurai who already had a master, but also illegal for such a person to then let that samurai go free. The punishment for this act was severe: "If you violate these laws and permit such a person to go free, three heads shall be cut off and dispatched to the previous master in place of that one man's head."

Years of Sengoku Period warfare had kept samurai away from their families in the provinces and ready for action, as each daimyō kept his army standing and battle-ready. But now their removal from the land and into the castle domain became a permanent requirement by law.

Edicts aside, Hideyoshi had higher aims than simply enacting a caste system in Japan. Buoyed by hubris and his success in Kyūshū, Hideyoshi was now preparing himself for another overseas

Right: Despite being Hideyoshi's heir, Toyotomi Hidetsugu was a cruel and hedonistic samurai who enjoyed killing in cold blood. Here, he meditates before committing seppuku.

campaign. As he had earlier told his wife, he intended to invade Korea and then China. This campaign, which ran between 1592 and 1596, is analyzed in greater detail in Chapter 2.

As his invasion of mainland Asia pressed on, Hideyoshi stayed in Japan, where, while waiting for news from Korea he spent much time watching Nō drama. Hideyoshi even wrote scripts for some theatres, often concerning his own exploits. In 1592, as his samurai landed in Korea, Hideyoshi took up the position of Taiko, or Retired Imperial Regent. This meant his heir, his nephew Hidetsugu, could become Regent. It was a move in name only, as in the true samurai tradition of cloistered rule, Hideyoshi retained complete control of all Japanese business from behind the scenes.

Despotic Regime

Hidetsugu himself was something of a disappointment, leading a reckless life as a teenager and developing a wayward reputation. The line of succession became confused in 1593 when one of Hideyoshi's mistresses gave birth to a son, Hideyori. Hideyoshi's absolute adoration and affection for Hideyori was in stark contrast to his public persona. For Hideyoshi the supreme ruler had become a despot. Many of his labourers were simply worked to death while building new residences and castles. This itself was perhaps

Right: A map detailing the territory won by Oda Nobunaga and Toyotomi Hideyoshi. It also shows Hideyoshi's campaigns in Japan and Korea.

not uncommon at the time, but Hideyoshi had also turned on friends and family. He forced his close confidant Sen no Rikyū, the innovator of the tea ceremony in Japan, to commit seppuku. The reason is unclear, but some say it was over a statue Rikyū ordered built of himself, which Hideyoshi considered vain.

Then Hideyoshi turned on Hidetsugu, his heir, known as the 'Murdering Regent' for killing innocents in cold blood. Hideyoshi banished Hidetsugu and then ordered him to commit seppuku. Next, Hideyoshi decided to ensure there would be no claimant to the title of Regent other than Hideyori. He stabbed to death Hidetsugu's three small children and over 30 women in his service. This was carried out in public, in the place where Hidetsugu's head was already on display. Citizens who spoke out about the murders were tortured and executed. The way now clear, Hideyori was appointed Regent at three years of age in 1596.

Hideyoshi was more or less deranged by the failure of his Korean campaign in 1594. He was enraged by the deception of his own men in incorrectly relaying the news and translating the taunting and threatening letters of rebuke from the Chinese Emperor. Hideyoshi ordered a reinvasion, this time not to conquer China but simply to punish the Koreans themselves. It was a pointless act that once again ended in defeat. In his grief and growing

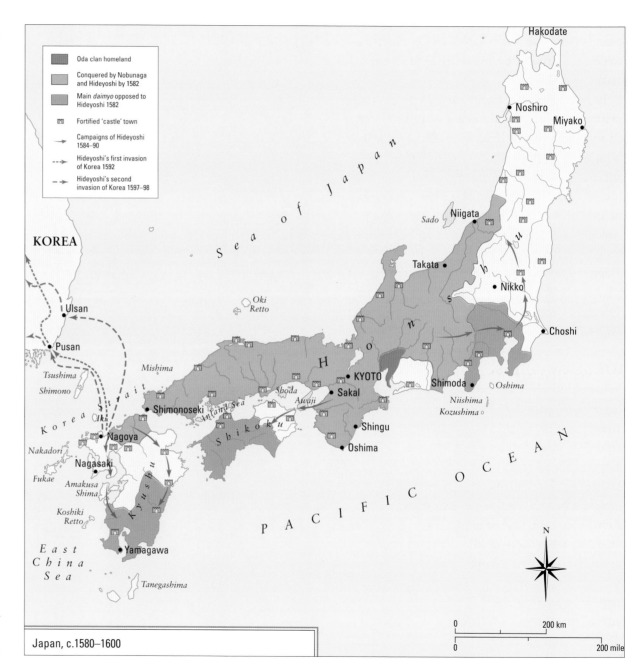

Japan, c.1580–1600

insanity Hideyoshi ordered that 26 Christians be executed by crucifixion as a warning to any who wished to convert.

In 1598 Hideyoshi took to his sick bed, where he become delirious and sometimes ordered that his attendants be beaten to death. Perhaps the only thing keeping Hideyoshi alive was his obsession with retaining Hideyori as Kampaku. To ensure this he created the Council of Five Elders, regents from the most powerful samurai houses – Togugawa, Maeda, Mori, Uyesugi and Ukita – and forced them to sign a declaration of allegiance to Hideyori. Hideyoshi made Ieyasu, in particular, swear an oath at his sick bed to reconfirm his declaration. It was Hideyoshi's last action before he died in his sleep a few days later.

TOKUGAWA IEYASU

Perhaps Ieyasu had had his fingers crossed when he swore at Hideyoshi's deathbed that he would ensure Hideyori's place as Regent. For not long after Hideyoshi's demise Ieyasu would be pronounced Shōgun of Japan and Hideyori would be dead. The political maneuvering for power began almost immediately after his demise. Two years of civil war ensued as the most powerful factions struggled for supreme control. On one side were the Toyotomi clan supporters, led by a samurai bureaucrat called Ishida Mitsunari, and on the other was Tokugawa Ieyasu.

Left: Tokugawa Ieyasu was the last of the three unifiers. Their roles are commonly described thus: 'Nobunaga mixed the cake, Hideyoshi baked it, Ieyasu ate it'.

Above: A scroll showing samurai dignitaries visiting Edo Castle. While Hideyoshi launched his disastrous Korean campaign, Ieyasu stayed behind to strengthen his domain of Edo.

Allies and Arrivals

The troops that allied themselves with Ishida Mitsunari and those who joined Tokugawa Ieyasu often came from very different ideologies. Mitsunari attracted disaffected Christians persecuted under the last years of Hideyoshi's rein. Ieyasu, on the other hand, welcomed ex-believers who had given up their faith. Hideyoshi and Ieyasu both persecuted Christians in Japan, starting with the Jesuit missionaries of Kyūshū. They also sought to crucify the crew of the crippled Dutch vessel the *Liefde*, which limped into Kyūshū in 1600 with a skeleton crew of sick and dying men. The captain, William Adams, became the first Englishman to set foot in Japan and was of great interest to Ieyasu, who invited him to his wartime residence, Ōsaka Castle. Adams was also asked to bring his cargo of 19 canons, 500 arquebuses, 5000 cannonballs, 300 chain shot and several tons of gunpowder – all a welcome addition to the Tokugawa arsenal. Adams, like all foreigners, was treated with caution and mistrust but he went on to become a member of Ieyasu's military entourage.

Right: William Adams was the first Englishman to set foot in Japan. Adams' cargo of firearms was of interest to Ieyasu, who made him a military advisor.

慶長拾四年七月日

布良人 ⊕

たらに船か以波濤付付之
浦、淮ぬ番津五ろ相遠ん
ん後守中百豆ま実咲中批役往業
御味そ舌ろ多家又ん作

Above: A Dutch trading pass from 1609. The Dutch obtained a special dispensation to trade with Japan even during its 'locked country' period.

Facing page: Sanada Yukimura is shown hiding at the Siege of Ōsaka. After failing to break through Yukimura's defences at Ōsaka, Ieyasu tried to bribe him instead.

Wealth and Status

In the time since his uprising against Hideyoshi, Ieyasu had quietly made himself the richest and most powerful daimyō in Japan, with a yearly income that dwarfed that of Hideyoshi himself. After their clash resulted in stalemate, Hideyoshi had allowed him to keep the five provinces of Mikawa, Tomomi, Suruga, Kai and Sinhano. This

was Hideyoshi's standard policy of appeasement for those who had risen against him, but he kept his eye on Ieyasu. He was a clear threat and his domains were dangerously close to Kyōto. Hideyoshi would solve this geographical issue after the 1590 Battle of Odawara. The conflict had freed up a vast swathe of confiscated land around the eastern province of Edo – a territory fit for a king, or at least a pretender to the throne. Moving Ieyasu to Edo was a clever move; it rewarded him for his demonstrated loyalty at Odawara while also removing him from his threatening central position.

Ieyasu was to greatly benefit from the move. Edo was a prosperous province, bursting with potential. He enlarged Edo's castle and undertook civic engineering works to improve the territory's infrastructure. He kept tight control over the peasantry surrounding his capital, and made sure his samurai had direct access to the best supplies and foodstuffs. While most daimyō were forced to commit troops to Hideyoshi's disastrous Korean campaign, Ieyasu managed to avoid it altogether. Instead he turned his attentions inward, making Edo strong and rich. By the time the bedraggled and battle-weary samurai returned from the Korean peninsula, Ieyasu had built himself a veritable empire with a revenue of over 2,500,000 koku a year. (A samurai's wealth was recorded in terms of their rice revenue, and one koku was the measure of rice needed to feed one man for a year.)

It is perhaps no wonder that Ieyasu had ideas about seizing power from the youngster Hideyori, and his ambitions would not end with the title of

Kampaku. Unlike the commoners Nobunaga and Hideyoshi, Ieyasu had noble Minamoto blood in his veins. This meant he could aspire to be the Shōgun itself, a position that in 1600 he had every intention of taking up. After months of clandestine meetings and cloaked alliances, Ishida Mitsunari cast the first stone by attacking Ieyasu's ally Torii Mototada in Hideyoshi's recently-built castle at Fushimi. So began a long series of skirmishes and sieges that would reach a climax on 21 October at the Battle of Sekigahara. The battle is analyzed in closer detail in the next chapter.

In the years following his victory at Sekigahara, Ieyasu consolidated his rule over the other daimyō of Japan. His allies were rewarded, but those who had opposed him or remained neutral lived difficult lives. His most trusted daimyō were handed territories where they could watch over those whom Ieyasu mistrusted the most. These daimyō were forced to build or pay for the construction of citadels, castles and other great buildings. In addition, restrictions were put on the size of their own fortresses and they were expected to spend a great deal of their time moving to and from the capital. With their fortifications, wealth and free time limited, usurping daimyōs had little option but to follow the Tokugawa line.

Meanwhile, Ieyasu was harvesting the fruits of his labour. His Sekigahara victory heralded not only his rise to the rank of Shōgun in 1603, but led to more than 250 years of Tokugawa rule. It ushered in the age known as the Edo Period, which would last until 1868.

Feudal and Social Divisions

Ieyasu continued Hideyoshi's policy of political reform, but issued his own series of edicts further dividing the classes along feudal lines. Samurai were to become a closed caste at the top of the social hierarchy and were expected to behave accordingly. Those with royal blood were also targeted. Iesayu's 1613 *Kuge Shohatto* document placed heavy restrictions on the Japanese nobility and all but limited their role to carrying out ceremonial functions. An even harsher document, the 1614 *Christian Expulsion Edict*, banned Christianity from being practised in Japan and forced all Christians and foreigners to leave the country.

In addition to his edicts, Ieyasu announced there would be 'no more wars', which in effect made the samurai – warriors who lived and died by the sword – redundant. As a result, Ieyasu started disbanding the clan armies in the provinces, leaving many samurai suddenly out of work. These unemployed samurai without a master to serve were called rōnin, or 'wave men'; destined to wander aimlessly, like the waves in the sea. To counter the rising tide of drifting rōnin, Ieyasu reluctantly allowed for samurai to take part in personal duels. Hundreds of thousands of rōnin wandered from town to town, looking for suitable opponents to test out their training and talents. A rōnin's first port of call upon entering a new town was its sword-fighting school, many of which sprang up around Japan during the Edo Period. Samurai warriors were handsomely paid to teach at these schools, although it was a risky vocation. If the master of a school lost a duel

with a traveling rōnin, he had to resign – assuming he was still alive.

Samurai duels were frequently fought to the death and were often anything but honourable; it was common for a group of samurai to lie in wait to ambush a single swordsman. But despite this, duelling between rōnin became so popular that Ieyasu moved to limit the growing number of fatalities by introducing two less harmful duelling swords. One was the bokken, made from solid wood, and the other was the shinai, made from bamboo slats. The shinai is still used today in the modern martial art of kendo. Beside officially sanctioned duels between samurai there were brawls and street fights. Incidents of this entirely dishonourable form of combat grew increasingly common during the Edo Period, and in an attempt to busy the peacetime samurai Ieyasu encouraged them to learn arts such as calligraphy and poetry, and to follow Buddhism. His encouragement was formalized in Iyeasu's *Buke Shohatto*, or 'Rules for Martial Families'. This was a strict code to govern samurai behaviour during times of peace and helped inform the formal codes of Bushidō published later in the Edo Period.

Taming the Samurai

The *Buke Shohatto* aimed to arm samurai warriors with a philosophical and cultivated outlook to replace their warmongering and desire for battle. In reality, many samurai gave up their swords to become bureaucrats, farmers and teachers, professions unthinkable to the warriors who had

come before them. Most samurai prayed for an outbreak of war or a local rebellion so that they could once again flex their sword-fighting muscles. One such opportunity presented itself in 1614, when Ieyasu's nemesis and one-time charge again reared his rebellious head.

While Ieyasu had spent the period after Sekigahara keeping daimyō weak and ineffectual, he had kept his best punishment for Hideyori himself. This was to rebuild Hideyoshi's great Buddha statue, which he began constructing from all of the weaponry confiscated during his 'great sword

Above: A bronze urn supposedly holding the last remains of Tokugawa Ieyasu, at the Tōshō-gū shrine in Nikkō, Tochigi Prefecture.

Facing page: A scroll depicting a rōnin duel from the Edo Period. Duels by masterless rōnin were such a frequent occurrence that they became punishable by seppuku.

hunt'. The statue had been partly completed at the time, but then destroyed during a 1596 earthquake. Hideyori's men had further bad luck when reconstructing the statue. At the point where only the head was left to attach, the statue of Buddha's body caught fire and burned to the ground. Work resumed a few years later, with 100,000 Toyotomi men involved in the statue's creation. It was also deemed that a great bronze bell be created to accompany the statue. But when the bell was completed it would set a series of events in motion that would sound the death knell

Buke Shohatto (The laws for the military houses)

1. Literature, arms, archery and horsemanship are, systematically, to be the favourite pursuits. Literature first, and arms next to it, was the rule of the ancients. They must both be cultivated concurrently. Archery and horsemanship are the more essential for the Military Houses… In times of peace and good order we must not forget that disturbances may arise. Dare we omit to practise our warlike exercises and drill?

2. Drinking parties and gaming amusements must be kept within due bounds.

3. Offenders against the law are not to be harboured in the (feudal) domain… To disregard the law (laid down by us) is an offence that will not be treated with leniency.

4. Throughout the domains whether of the greater or lesser Barons or of the holders of minor benefices, if any of the gentry or soldiers in their service be guilty of rebellion or murder, such offenders must be at once expelled from their domain.

5. Henceforth no social intercourse is to be permitted outside of one's own domain, with the people (gentry and commoners) of another domain.

6. The residential castles in the domains may be repaired, but the matter must invariably be reported. Still more imperative is it that the planning of structural innovations of any kind must be absolutely avoided. A castle with a parapet exceeding 100 chi is a bane to a domain. Crenelated walls and deep moats (of castles) are the causes of anarchy.

7. If in a neighbouring domain innovations are being hatched or cliques being formed the fact is to be reported without delay.

8. Marriages must not be contracted at private convenience.

9. As to the rule that the daimyōs shall come (to the Shōgun's Court at Yedo) to do service.

10. There must be no confusion in respect of dress uniforms, as regards the materials thereof. The distinction between lord and vassal, between superior and inferior, must be clearly marked by the apparel… In recent times retainers and henchmen (soldiers) have taken to wearing rich damasks and silk brocade. This elaborate display was not allowed by the ancient laws and it must be severely kept within bounds.

11. Miscellaneous persons are not at their own pleasure to ride in palanquins. There are families who for special reasons from of old have inherited the privilege of riding in palanquins without permission from the authorities… But, latterly, even sub-vassals and henchmen of no rank have taken to so riding. This is a flagrant impertinence.

12. The samurai throughout the provinces are to practise frugality. Those who are rich like to make a display, whilst those who are poor are ashamed of not being on a par with the others. There is no other influence so pernicious to social observances as this, and it must be strictly kept in check.

13. The lords of the great domains must select men of capacity for office. The way to govern a country is to get hold of the proper men. The merits and demerits (of retainers) should be closely scanned, and reward or reproof unflinchingly distributed accordingly.

Keicho,
20th year, 7th month
(24 August–23 September 1615).

Right: A samurai demonstrates sword stances with his drawn katana. By holding his sword upright in this way, it was easy for a samurai to commit to a cut or parry an opponent's blow.

for Hideyori. The problem was not with the bell itself, but rather the inscription: 'May the state be peaceful and prosperous", which split the ideographs 'Ie' and 'yasu' in half. This coincidental sundering of his name incensed Ieyasu. There was a further outrage when an inscription on the bell mentioned bidding farewell to 'the setting sun', which the septuagenarian took as a thinly veiled reference to him.

There were also reports that Hideyori had been harbouring the victims of Ieyau's policies in his castle at Ōsaka. These were Christians, rōnin and other malcontents, who probably felt they had little left to lose. The resulting siege of Ōsaka Castle, discussed in detail in Chapter 2, was the last warring victory of Ieyasu's life.

Unlike his two great unifying counterparts – Nobunaga and Hideyoshi – Ieyasu's hold on Japan would remain in place for centuries. The Edo Period represented 250 years of peace in Japan under the Tokugawa Shōgunate. Outliving all of the three unifiers is a Japanese saying that describes their roles: 'Nobunaga mixed the cake, Hideyoshi baked it, Ieyasu ate it'. But for Ieyasu there was little time to enjoy the period of peace following the Siege of Ōsaka Castle. He was taken ill the following year and died in 1616. It was said he grasped his sword until the end.

Battles of the Samurai

The battles of the Sengoku Jidai represented a revolution in samurai warfare. Before then, battles were fought according to centuries-old traditions that emphasized ritual, honour and individual prowess in combat.

Mounted samurai would call out their family name and achievements to attract an enemy warrior of similar standing. A duel with bows and arrows would follow, which sometimes stopped the battle in its tracks as warriors from either side paused to watch. If a winner had not been decided, both opponents would dismount and carry on with their swords. The defeated party would be permitted to commit sepukku before being decapitated – if this had not already happened. The head would then be attached to a board with a spike for the 'viewing of the heads ceremony' after battle. Each head would have a tag to identify the warrior and the name of the samurai responsible for the beheading. Medieval

Facing page: The Siege of Ōsaka was the last time two samurai armies fought a pitched battle. The outcome would secure Ieyasu's position as Shōgun of Japan.

Right: Beheading was the customary way for a samurai to finish off an enemy warrior. Here, a collection of enemy heads are exhibited on bamboo stalks.

texts painted the heroic deeds of samurais with broad, romantic strokes. These were the aristocratic duelists who fought other gentlemen of war by consent. Supporting their master's every needs were armed attendants who also dealt with some of the less civilized aspects of war – arson, surprise attacks, night raids, collection of the heads and so forth. But by the mid-sixteenth century, samurai warfare had moved away from the deeds of individual warriors to the strategies and tactics of large troop movements on the battlefield.

Samurai warfare had, to an extent, always moved with the times. Battles were usually won by bringing the greatest number of mounted samurai down. But duels between samurai gentlemen were not an efficient method of improving one side's head count. A simpler method was to have a gang of foot soldiers attack one samurai en masse, and unhorse him with naginatas, a type of polearm with a long, curved blade. The naginata was the first great battlefield leveller, giving an armed attendant the chance to be victorious against his social better attacking

from on high. In response to increasing foot soldier attacks, the mounted samurai abandoned his bow for the straight spear, the preferred weapon of choice throughout the Sengoku Jidai.

Infantry Firepower

The role of the armed attendant on the battlefield was to become all-important by the mid-sixteenth century. Once a peasant recruited from the fields of a samurai clan's domain, fighting attendants would become trained foot soldiers called ashigaru. The ashigaru would be armed with the great technological wonder of the Sengoku Jidai – the arquebus. The Portuguese arquebus had landed on Japanese shores in 1543 and quickly became a major game-changer on the field of conflict. Although its matchlock mechanism made it slow to load and tricky to aim for any distance, a number of the weapons fired from the front line of an army could bring down an enemy charge. Like the naginata before it, the arquebus was a battlefield leveller: an ashigaru could be trained to fire one in a day to bring down a mounted samurai aristocrat who had spent his life studying the art of warfare.

Ashigaru became so important that from the time of the Tokugawa Shōgunate they would make up the lower ranks of the samurai class. Their place in the hierarchy, however, was always made clear – they would have lower-quality armour and wear a jingasa war hat instead of a kabuto helmet and facemask. Ashigaru would also not have surnames, although up until 1615 it was possible to acquire one and move through the ranks to become a

Below: Ashigaru were the low-ranking foot soldiers of a samurai army. The ashigaru shown here carry katanas and yaris, but they were also often armed with arquebuses.

samurai proper. The most famous ashigaru who achieved this upward social mobility was the man who passed a law forbidding any other ashigaru to do the same – Toyotomi Hideyoshi. The evolving role of ashigaru as a trained soldier represented a change in Sengoku Jidai warfare, as warring clans were replaced with samurai armies. Ashigaru would lead the forward lines of these armies, which were positioned into formations and moved like chess pieces around the field of conflict. The formations were given names, such as 'Birds in Flight', 'Fish Scales' and 'Stork's Wing'.

Most battles were fought between the armies of allied clans led by a commander-in-chief who had prearranged the battle plan with his opposite number. At the top of each army's hierarchy were mounted samurai spearmen, followed by samurai retainers on foot, who were in turn supported by ashigaru. Ashigaru were divided into contingents armed with spears, arquebuses and bows and arrows. Some of these ashigaru were responsible for guarding a large detachment of flag bearers. Each commander-in-chief would also be surrounded by a personal bodyguard, a microcosm of the larger army that featured samurai horsemen, retainers on foot, flag-bearers, and spear, bow and arrow, and arquebus ashigaru.

The commander and his bodyguard would set up a command post at a good vantage point to the battle, usually on a hill or at the base of a mountain.

Ieyasu's Field Orders

Ieyasu had specific ideas about his men's conduct in war. The following are his field orders for the 1590 Siege of Odawara:

1. If anyone advances and reconnoitres without orders he shall be punished.

2. Anyone who presses too far forward, even though to make a name for himself… will be punished with all his family.

3. Anyone who is found trespassing in another company without reason shall be deprived of his horse and arms.

4. When troops are on the march none shall go by byways… If any move in a disorderly fashion their leader will be held culpable.

5. Anyone who disobeys the orders of the Bugyō will be punished.

6. When troops are on the march, all flags, guns, bows and spears are to be carried according to fixed order… Any disorder will be punished.

7. Except when in the ranks it is forbidden to go about carrying long spears.

8. Anyone letting a horse stray in the camp will be punished.

9. As to the baggage train, strict orders are to be given that they are to be allotted a proper place so they do not get mixed with the troops. Any who do will be put to death on the spot.

10. Without orders no one may seize any man or woman and take them. Should anyone take and conceal any such person his master shall correct the

Above: Ieyasu's armies were strictly controlled: dissent or disobedience were punishable by death.

matter… And the vanguard shall not, without orders, set fire to any house in enemy territory.

11. Violence and intimidation of tradespeople is strictly forbidden. Offenders will be put to death on the spot.

12. Anyone who strikes camp without orders will be punished.

So be it.

Tensho 18 February 1591

Ieyasu

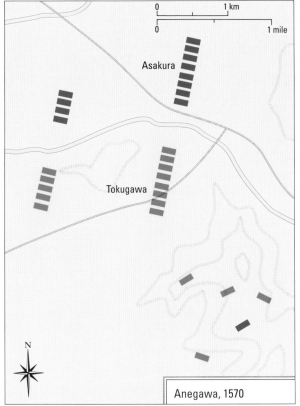

Above: The 1570 Battle of Anegawa pitted for the first time an alliance of Oda Nobunaga and Tokugawa Ieyasu against the combined forces of the Azai and Asakura clans. It resulted in a victory for the new alliance.

Right: Tokugawa Ieyasu's favourite pastimes were falconry and swimming. But despite these active pursuits, he grew portly in his later life.

Here the commander would sit on a camp stool and be hidden from view by a maku, a type of high-walled tent without a roof. The commander stayed on his stool for the viewing of the heads ceremony, which followed the conclusion of battle.

Tokugawa Ieyasu warned that it was a mistake 'to think that battles can be won sitting on a camp stool giving orders', and often gave his while sitting on horseback. Commanders used a baton or fan to issue their orders to those on the battlefield, which were used in conjunction with drums and gongs. A first order would often signal a detachment of mounted samurai to coax a detachment on the opposite side to chase them. When this happened, the enemy pursuers often found themselves charging into a line of arquebus-firing ashigaru and archers. These firing lines would then fall back so that lines of ashigaru armed with spears could charge. As the forward units fought, divisions made up of samurai cavalry would attack the enemy flanks. Other divisions were kept back to launch surprise attacks at pivotal moments. This tactic, famously adopted at the Battle of Sekigahara, would often lead to treachery and opportunism among the so-called samurai allies.

The trick for any commander was to keep his armies together in battle formation for as long as possible. Sooner or later the samurai spirit of individualism and personal glory would take hold, the ranks would break and a melee would follow. This was no-holds barred, hand-to-hand combat, as samurai from every different class would hack, slice and blast at each other.

Pitched battles only made up half of the warfare commonly seen during the later stages of the Sengoku Jidai. The introduction of the arquebus to the battlefield had led to the construction of large stone fortresses to withstand them. Unlike Europe at the same time in history, firearms did not lead to the end of castle-building, but rather to the beginning of it. While arquebuses became the mainstay of samurai armies, cannons did not take on in the same way. The most effective cannons were those imported from Europe, while Japanese models were best known for making a lot of noise but not much real damage.

Attrition Warfare

As more castles were built to deal with the increasing arquebus threat, so did the numbers of sieges. Sieges became commonplace during the late Sengoku Jidai, as samurai armies chose to hide out rather than meet their opponents in a pitched battle. Sieges were, however, a last resort. For the defenders, it was usually only a matter of time before starvation and disease overcame their best efforts to hold out. But if the defenders had large enough stores of rice and a well within the castle, as was the case during the Siege of Ōsaka, their lives could be considerably more comfortable than those of the attackers outside.

Attacking a strong castle such as Ōsaka was a tedious and unrewarding business. Winter could see the attacking army face starvation, or at the very least become bored and rebellious. Common methods of attack were full-frontal assaults using

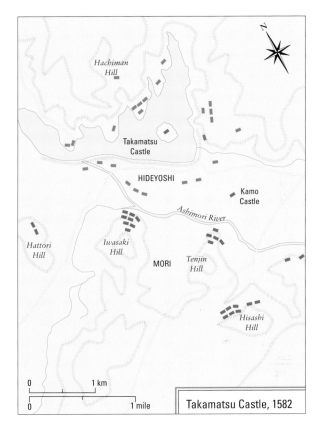

Above: Hideyoshi's 1582 siege of Takamatsu Castle would involve him diverting the waters from two nearby rivers to flood the defenders out.

Facing page: Honda Tadatomo, wearing his standard helmet adorned with deer antlers, leads the Tokugawa attack against the defenders of Ōsaka Castle.

Above: Yoshimitsu was a Minamoto hero of the twelfth century Gempei War. The sixteenth century Takeda clan could trace its lineage to the Minamoto.

Facing page: Torii Suneemon was given a choice at the walls of Nagashino Castle: betray those inside and live, or stay loyal to the defenders and die.

bamboo scaling ladders and siege towers, from which arquebuses could be fired over the fortress walls. Undermining to bring down an outer wall was often used, but impractical against a castle with a wet moat. In the end, great generals on the field, such as Ieyasu himself, would make the royal residences within a castle the main target. In such cases any notion of honourable warfare, so revered in the epic texts of medieval samurai heroes, were forgotten.

The four battles featured in this chapter represent samurai warfare at its absolute peak, its methods tried, tested and perfected on the battlefield. Its martial ethos is less obvious, as betrayal, deceit and entirely dishonourable conduct were common. The battles would feature the largest samurai armies ever put together in Japanese history. They led, however, to 250 years of peace under one Shōgunate – and also to the long, slow demise of the samurai themselves.

BATTLE OF NAGASHINO

Nagashino has all the hallmarks of a legendary Japanese battle: warfare against impossible odds, betrayal, hubris, doomed cavalry charges and the tragic recklessness of vainglorious young generals, all wrapped up in a hopeless power struggle that would spell the end for an entire clan.

It was also the battle that marked a sea-change in the way Japanese warfare was fought. The established order of mounted samurai was doomed when it confronted lines of ashigaru foot soldiers armed with arquebuses. Representing this established order was the Takeda, one of Japan's oldest and most powerful clans. Takeda samurai could trace their ancestry to ninth-century Emperor Seiwa and the hero of the Gempei War, Minamoto no Yoshimitsu. Opposing the Takeda was the young gekokujō upstart Oda Nobunaga, who had no aristocratic lineage, nor any chance of uniting Japan without first destroying his great Takeda rival. Nobunaga, however, was only a secondary character in this epic conflict. Taking centre stage in his place was the tragic Takeda Katsuyori, the arrogant and impetuous daimyō condemned not only to live in his father's shadow but also to pour ruin upon the Takeda clan. His father was the formidable Takeda Shingen, a man whose very name sent shivers up Oda Nobunaga's spine.

Shingen was the daimyō who had destroyed Tokugawa Ieyasu's samurai on the plain of Mikatagahara by crashing through his front line with a courageous cavalry charge. But soon after Mikatagahara, Shingen had come undone. While besieging Ieyasu's Noda Castle in 1573, he was killed by an extraordinarily lucky arquebus shot from the fortresses walls. His dying wish was that the Takeda keep his demise a secret for three years.

Katsuyori and his uncle Nobukado put the period of this deception to good use by waging a series of campaigns against Ieyasu and Oda Nobunaga. Katsuyori, in particular, initiated a number of raids into Ieyasu's provinces of Tomoti and Mikawa, which culminated in the capture of Takatenjin Castle – an illustrious victory for the new daimyō.

Takatenjin Castle made a good starting-point for Katsuyori, but it wasn't his intended destination. Instead, he wanted to use it as a steppingstone on the path to Okazaki Castle in Mikawa. Okazaki was the capital city and the jewel in the crown of Mikawa province. If it fell, Ieyasu's powerbase would be severely undermined, while Katsuyori's would strengthen considerably. And Katsuyori had a spy on the inside who had promised to throw open the castle doors to let the Takeda samurai in.

Nagashino Castle Siege

Unfortunately for Katsuyori the plot was discovered and the traitor executed. This news caught up with Katsuyori's army at the midway point on its march to Okazaki. Here, his army pulled up sharply by

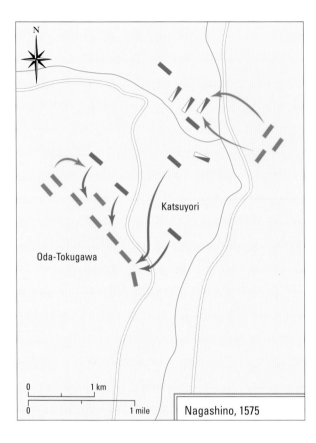

Above: The 1575 Battle of Nagashino ended in a bloody victory for Nobunaga, as waves of Takeda cavalry charges crashed onto his fortified lines of arquebus-armed ashigaru.

Facing page: This scene from Akira Kurosawa's *Kagemusha* depicts the doomed Takeda cavalry charge at the Battle of Nagashino. Over 5000 extras were used to film the scene.

the frontier castle of Nagashino. It is unclear if Katsuyori actually had designs on Nagashino or whether it simply presented itself as the closest enemy target after Okazaki fell out of the running. Whatever his rationale, Katsuyori decided his 15,000-strong samurai army would be allowed to cut their teeth on Nagashino Castle. The castle itself was built on a rocky outcrop next to the joining of two rivers. Its position made it easy to defend, but the garrison of 500 samurai inside the castle was not equipped to withstand a long siege. After a few fruitless assaults against the castle walls, Katsuyori decided to dig himself in and starve the inhabitants out.

Katsuyori's men pitched camp on a plain to the north of the castle, and surrounded the fortress with palisades and ditches to prevent an easy exodus. Rope barriers and nets were then strung across and through the rivers to the south and east of the castle to prevent an escape, or attack, by boat. So it was that Nagashino Castle was caught in Katsuyori's trap, seemingly with no way in or out, or any means to alert Ieyasu or Nobunaga to its peril. Nobunaga and Ieyasu, however, had already received news of Nagashino's plight and had met at Okazaki to decide their strategy. But their conference was interrupted by Torii Suneemon, a samurai retainer who had escaped from Nagashino Castle. Suneemon had managed to slip out of the castle under cover of night and swim downstream by cutting through the Takeda nets with a dagger. He then ran the 40km (25 miles) or so to Okazaki with crucial news: the castle defences were intact,

but the defenders had only enough food and water to last a few days. Nobunaga lost no time readying his army to march on Nagashino, and ordered Torii Suneemon back to the castle to relay this news. But during Suneemon's absence the Takeda had discovered what he had done and replaced the cut nets with a stronger trip-wires and roped webbing. This time, as Suneemon approached the castle, he was caught.

Katsuyori tried to bargain with Suneemon for his life. He was mounted onto a cross that was tall enough to reach the castle walls, and told to lie about Nobunaga's approach. If he convinced the castle to surrender, Suneemon would live. A long spear was held under the retainer's ribs as an extra incentive. But when the cross was raised up to the battlements, Torii yelled out for the castle to hold tight, Nobunaga was on his way. This moment of heroism was predictably Suneemon's final act. For the besieged inside the castle, the cat was out of the bag.

But Suneemon's news had also alerted Katsuyori to Nobunaga's imminent arrival. Now he had a choice: retreat from what would certainly be a perilously large Oda force, or stand his ground and fight like a true Takeda great. Those opposed to open battle were Katsuyori's 'Twenty-Four Generals' – his father's former military advisors who had won many military victories for the Takeda. But agitating for war was an impetuous young general called Atobe Oinosuke. Oinosuke maligned his military elders and swore that Takeda samurai never turned their backs on an approaching army. The sentiment appealed to Katsuyori, who wanted to build his reputation for

Above: A modern recreation of the Battle of Nagashino stands on the plain of Shitarabara. In view are the palisades which protected the Oda arquebusiers.

Facing page: Oda Nobunaga used three lines of arquebusiers to deliver rotating volleys of fire at Nagashino. The tactic would change the face of samurai warfare.

heroism. The fledging daimyō was all too aware of how paltry his accomplishments were when compared with his father's.

The Twenty-Four Generals also disagreed with their younger counterparts over the Takeda battle plan. Nobunaga was at the head of a 30,000-strong samurai army, and marching with him was Iesayu

and his supplementary force of 8000 samurai. Katsuyori, who led 15,000 samurai, would be badly outnumbered in a pitched battle on the plain. The Twenty-Four Generals suggested they mount another offensive against Nagashino Castle. Even if 1000 men were sacrificed in the assault, the castle would at least provide a stronghold for their outnumbered army. They reasoned that Nobunaga would not lay siege forever, and sooner or later they would be able to regain their freedom. But once again Oinosuke demurred. Had the generals ever heard of Nobunaga retreating? And what would they prefer – dying of starvation in a keep, or battling it out like warriors on the plain? Thus the argument was resolved. Katsuyori would stake everything on a pitched battle to be fought on the plain of Shitarabara, north of Nagashino Castle.

The Battle

While Nobunaga's approaching army outnumbered Katsuyori's, it would be wrong to assume the day would be lost on these grounds alone. This was going to be a battle of wits as much as muscle, and in his preparations Katsuyori was as careful in playing to his army's strengths as Nobunaga was to his. This was Katsuyori's rationale in positioning himself for a pitched battle. It would enable a Takeda cavalry charge across the open country towards the Oda front line. The tactic had worked to devastating effect against Ieyasu at Mikatagahara, although it was not Katsuyori but his father who had won the battle on that occasion.

Nobunaga had anticipated Katsuyori would attempt a cavalry charge even before he had marched from Okazaki. For this reason he had picked out 3000 arquebus marksmen from among his ashigaru to lead the assault. Then, when Nobunaga reached the plain of Shitarabara, he ordered his men to build palisades around 2.1m (7ft) high along a front line. These would stop

Right: A general oversees his troops attack at the Battle of Nagashino, as imagined by Japanese artist Taiso Yoshitoshi (1887).

a mounted attack, but at the same time provide cover through which the ashigaru could fire their arquebuses. But there was to be more than just a single line of arqubusiers. There would be three lines of soldiers delivering rotating volleys of fire. Between each stockade was a space of several metres through which Nobunaga's men could launch a counterattack. In a way, Nobunaga's tactic was a type of blitzkrieg from the ground. His ashigaru would rain a hail of musket shot on to the charging ranks, and then samurai swordsmen would mop up any stragglers who were left standing. It was to be a brilliant but brutally clever turn.

The morning of 21 June 1585 was dry and clear after a night of heavy rain. Takeda Katsuyori had reasonably expected that Nobunaga's men would have been unable to keep their arquebus gunpowder dry overnight, rendering their weapons useless. There was certainly no discernable sign of activity from behind the palisades, and at dawn the whole plain was eerily silent. Nobunaga ordered around 2000 samurai to march outside the palisades to draw the Takeda in. The tactic worked. Two detachments of Takeda cavalry charged on Nobunaga's samurai to the left and right of the palisade lines. This was marginally successful, as the Takeda horsemen managed to break through the samurai lines on the left. Buoyed by this success Katsuyori ordered another charge, this time on the

centre of the palisade line itself. The daimyō must have anticipated some initial losses to arquebus fire, but was gambling that there would be enough strength in the Takeda line to break through the wooden palisades. What he hadn't counted on was the rotating volley of fire, which cut through the lines of cavalry before they had even reached the fortifications.

Battlefield Victory

Katsuyori countered by sending most of his samurai in another charge directly at the palisades. The cavalry charges came first, followed by lines of foot soldiers. It was a bloodbath. The horses were mown down and those samurai who had survived engaged in hand-to-hand combat with Nobunaga retainers streaming out from between the palisades. Over 10,000 Takeda men went down in this way. A stunned Katsuyori and his advisors were forced to admit defeat and flee for their lives. The Takeda had been totally outdone by the Nobunaga's tactics, which had proved beyond any doubt that the arquebus now ruled supreme over the samurai battlefield. The aristocratic Takeda, with their outdated notions of heroic samurai on horseback, had been destroyed by a gekokujō general and his ashigaru shooters. Samurai warfare would never be the same again.

THE KOREAN WAR

It was a sign of Hideyoshi's burgeoning megalomania that he made plans to invade China in 1587, three years before he had even finished the more pressing task of unifying Japan. Once he had done so, however, Hideyoshi began amassing arms, armies, and ships to begin an invasion in earnest. His plan was simple: to land his force of 160,000 samurai in Korea in divisional waves. Then, once Korea had been taken, he would send reinforcements of another 170,000 samurai to invade China. After that, Hideyoshi would push forward to the Indian subcontinent. Bringing China to its knees would take around a year, Hideyoshi explained to his then heir, Hidetsugu.

Standing in the way of Japan and the mighty Ming Dynasty – the military family responsible for ousting the Mongols – was, of course, Korea. But Hideyoshi planned to offer the Koreans a deal: in return for allowing his army to move freely through their country, they would become part of his flourishing kingdom. The problem was that Korea was a vassal state of imperial China, so his offer to challenge the Chinese overlord was scarcely appealing. There was also the difficult issue of freedom of movement, something that Korea was not keen to provide. Spain and Portugal had also declined Hideyoshi's invitation to join the fray. Spain had sent a globe highlighting the many territories currently under its dominion, and Portugal could not see the benefit of putting a fleet of warships at Hideyoshi's disposal. While the subtleties of these replies were probably lost on Hideyoshi, one thing was clear: Japan would have to carry out its invasion alone. Luckily for Hideyoshi, he would not personally have to pay for it. Neither would those closest to him. Instead, those daimyō who

The Takeda End

The epilogue to the Battle of Nagashino focuses on the fate of Katsuyori and the Takeda clan, and it ends not with a bang but a whimper. Nagashino was far from a decisive blow for Nobunaga. It took six years for him to reclaim Takatenjin Castle from the Takeda, and in that time Katsuyori had built himself the new fortress of Shimpujo. But Shimpujo would not stand for long. A combined push by Oda and Tokugawa forces aimed to finish the Takeda once and for all. As their armies invaded Takeda territories, Katsuyori's allies dropped out of the campaign. The daimyō's popularity had waned following Nagashino and the construction of Shimpujo, and by 1582 Katsuyori was short of friends. Nobunaga and Ieyasu responded by hunting down the weak and isolated daimyō. Time and again Katsuyori was forced to fight and retreat. Finally he was left with only a bodyguard of a few hundred retainers. By then, Katsuyori's family had retreated to a Takeda stronghold, leaving the daimyō to fend for himself as the Oda and Tokugawa closed in. The end came on a mountain pass called Toriibata, where only a handful of Takeda stayed to fight. As this remnant struggled, Katsuyori and his wife and son committed sepukku. With them, the Takeda line came to its tragic end.

Right: Japan is an archipelago of 6852 islands separated from Korea by the treacherous Sea of Japan. The sea has a history of storms and shipwrecks.

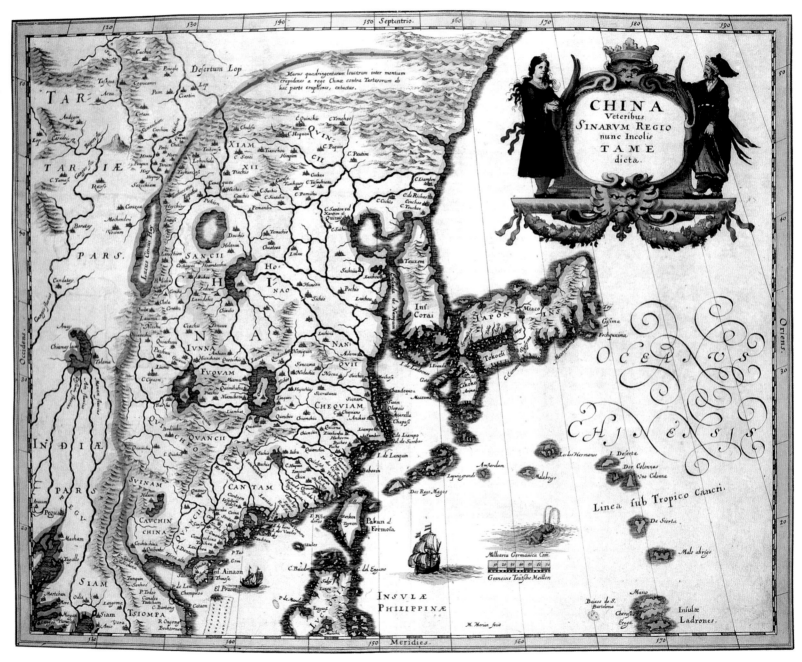

The Main Commanders

JAPAN

Konishi Yukinaga

The daimyō of Uto in Kyūshū, Yukinaga was a Jesuit convert who fought against Ieyasu in the 1600 Battle of Sekigahara. Yukinaga was the first to land in Korea and the last to leave.

Katō Kiyomasa

Kiyomasa was a Buddhist, a military purist and something of an eccentric. He wore an unkempt beard supposedly to stop the straps of his helmet chafing him, and believed that any samurai interested in dance should be forced to commit seppuku.

KOREA

Yi Sun-sin

Yi Sun-sin was Korea's greatest naval commander who took his first command at the age of 31. After being stripped of his rank, demoted to foot soldier and then reinstated, Admiral Yi was to prove pivotal in battling the Japanese at sea.

CHINA

Li Rusong

The Commander-in-Chief of the Chinese army, Li was responsible for several victories against the Japanese and helped enable their expulsion from Korea.

Left: Konishi Yukinaga was the first general to land in Korea in 1592. He would race rival daimyō Katō Kiyomasa to conquer the city of Seoul.

Right: Korean admiral Yi Sun-sin was Korea's great naval hero. His ships would break up the samurai supply lines and make an occupation of Korea impossible.

Right: The Japanese invasion of Korea. The first division was led by Konishi Yukinaga, the second by Katō Kiyomasa, and the third by Kuroda Nagamasa. The fourth division combined elements of the other three.

had opposed Hideyoshi, and those nearest to the invasion's launch point in Kyūshū, would be forced to supply the necessary samurai and resources.

Hideyoshi's plan was to dispatch the first division under Konishi Yukinaga, the second under Katō Kiyomasa and the third division under Kuroda Nagamasa. The problem was that Yukinaga and Kiyomasa hated each other – both were also rivals of Nagamasa, a condition not untypical of samurai generals in the field. Hideyoshi himself never went to Korea. The Invasion of Korea, therefore, turned into a no-holds-barred race to take Seoul and then P'yongyang. The collateral damage was to the Korean nation, whose people were butchered in masses.

Konishi Yukinaga was the first to land his force at the main Korean port of Pusan on 24 May 1592. The Japanese armada had been sighted the previous day, and the signal beacon had been lit to warn those in Seoul. The occupants of Pusan had waited to receive orders via signal beacon in return, but none had come. The greatest irony of the invasion is that the technologically advanced Korean navy could have made short work of the vastly inferior Japanese ships if given the order to sail out in time. But this was typical of the Koreans, whose preparations for the Japanese invasion had been lacklustre at best.

Invasion of Korea, 1592,
and the retreat to Seoul, 1593

→ First division

---→ Second division

······► Third division

—·—► Fourth division

Massacre at Pusan

When the samurai leapt from their ships at Pusan, the Korean force charged with protecting the fortified city seemed genuinely surprised that the warriors were firing at them with arquebuses. This was despite Hideyoshi sending several of the weapons with his delegation to ask for Korean participation. The predictable outcome at Pusan, therefore, was a bloodbath. The samurai went forward in waves, lines of arquebus-armed ashigaru to start, followed by lines of samurai swordsmen. The men, women and children of Pusan begged for mercy as they were hacked down indiscriminately. When the news reached Seoul, it came with reports of cats and dogs being included in the mass beheadings.

The plan was for Konishi Yukinaga to stay in Pusan and wait for Katō Kiyomasa's arrival with the second division. But instead, Yukinaga marched directly to Seoul. Kiyomasa landed in Korea two days later. He was furious at the bad weather that had hampered his arrival, and his mood was made worse when he heard that Yukinaga's army was already travelling north.

In 1592 there were three roads that led from Pusan in the south to Seoul in the middle of Korea,

Right: The Panokseon was a Korean warship powered by both oars and sails. Its multiple decks provided platforms for attack as well protection for the oarsmen.

Korean Weaponry

The Korean army was underequipped to deal with the superior Japanese force in virtually every respect. Korean soldiers carried short, double-edged swords, straight spears and a type of mace on a long pole. They also used specially designed weapons that consisted of several firing tubes attached together. These could dispatch a volley of steel-tipped arrows further than an archer's bow and were deadly on the battlefield. The arrow-launchers, combined with Chinese cannon and mortar, were the pride of the Korean artillery, and about the only thing it could be proud of. Unfortunately, there were not enough of these weapons to enable the Koreans to withstand an invading force.

Facing page: A samurai warrior fords a river on horseback. The Korean Imjin River stopped the samurai advance on the city of P'yongyang in its tracks.

and there was a samurai army on each one speeding towards the capital. Resistance to the Japanese had been rare. The battle-hardened warriors overran any town or citadel that stood in their way, slaughtering the Korean inhabitants as they went.

Despite his tardy start to the campaign, Katō Kiyomasa was sure he had beaten Yukinaga to Seoul when he approached the capital on 12 June. From a distance the city seemed devoid of life. Unfortunately for Kiyomasa, Yukinaga's army had arrived a few hours earlier to find Seoul's gates thrown open and the city abandoned. Among the terrified residents travelling north to P'yongyang was the Korean king and his imperial coffers. Many royal buildings were set alight as he left. The jewel in the Korean crown was now P'yongyang.

But between the samurai forces led by Konishi Yukinaga and Katō Kiyomasa was the natural barrier of the Imjin River, with 10,000 Korean soldiers protecting the banks of its far side. This stopped the Japanese in their tracks. There was simply no way across unless the Koreans could be moved. But through sheer gullibility the Koreans would move themselves, falling for the oldest samurai trick in the book.

After 10 days, Yukinaga and Kiyomasa simply broke camp on their side of the river and pretended to retreat south. The Korean generals then ordered a pursuit, only to walk into an ambush of arquebus fire. The result was a rout and a massacre. The Japanese divisions then split, Konishi Yukinaga marching on P'yongyang and Katō Kiyomasa on the peninsula's northeastern territories.

Another river, the Tadong, lay between Kiyomasa and P'yongyang, and again it was protected by a contingent of the Korean army. This time, Yukinaga tried the diplomatic route. He met the Korean general on a boat at the midway point of the river and said Japan only wanted peace – and safe passage through P'yongyang to the Chinese border. After the slaughter of thousands of innocent Koreans it was a hard argument to swallow, and the next morning the Korean army attacked Yukinaga's camp. Once again the Koreans proved they were no match for the samurai in open battle, and this time they had made the mistake of showing the enemy where to ford the river. Within a few hours, Yukinaga's men were standing in the deserted city of P'yongyang.

The Tide Turns

Just north of P'yongyang lay China, the country that Hideyoshi had hoped would be his within a matter of months. Ecstatic at the news about P'yongyang, he had written to his heir Hidetsugu telling him to pack a bag for China and that 'five suits of armour should be enough'. In addition, Hideyoshi ordered a force of 50,000 samurai reserves to sail along the west coast of Korea and bolster Yukinaga's army. But the invasion of P'yongyang was going to be the end of the good news for Hideyoshi. In the event, not one Japanese soldier would cross the border into China, for while the samurai had been winning victories on land, they had not been so successful at sea.

After the initial inaction of the Korean navy, Admiral Yi had taken command of the sea

The Korean Navy

Apart from hoping the Portuguese would send warships to help with the invasion, Hideyoshi had given little thought to the naval campaign. The Japanese navy was made up mostly of transport ships and some 'warships' that were really just transport ships with extra samurai onboard. The Korean navy, by comparison, was a formidable fleet, led by the iron-clad 'Geobukseon' or 'turtleships'.

Turtleships were around 30m (98ft) long and 9m (29ft) wide, powered by a sail and oars. The deck was not exposed, but covered by curved planks of wood in the style of a turtle shell, making it difficult to attack. Along each side were 20 cannon firing 3m- (10ft-) long steel-tipped projectiles, giant flaming arrows or shot. The shell of the turtleship was covered in iron cladding with iron spikes to further deter boarding parties.

When a turtleship moved into an attack position, the mast would fold away into the deck and yellow smoke would billow out of the mouth of a dragon's head at the boat's prow. The yellow fog would literally provide a smokescreen that confused the enemy and kept the turtleship's position a mystery.

Right: While the Japanese proved militarily stronger on the ground they were no match for the unfamiliar turtleships of the Korean navy.

campaign. This he carried out with remarkable aplomb: hundreds of transport and supply ships had been sunk, and almost 10,000 Japanese samurai lost. Yi had also managed to cut off the sea route to the Korean north. This meant no reinforcements would reach P'yongyang, and vital supplies needed by samurai around Korea would end up on the ocean floor. To make matters worse, a Chinese army was on its way to P'yongyang.

As the Chinese marched towards P'yongyang they were surprised to see the gates of the city left open. Could it be the Japanese had retreated south without a fight? No: Yukinaga's men had lured their enemy into another trap. Once the Chinese army entered the city the samurai leapt from their hiding places and overcame the enemy. But it was a warning to both the Chinese and Yukinaga. Thanks to the work of Admiral Yi, supplies were getting low in P'yongyang and the samurai were feeling the pinch. Korean guerillas south of the city, moreover, had launched a counterattack. Thousands of displaced Korean soldiers were disrupting supply lines, raiding samurai strongholds and in some cases retaking whole cities. On 6 September, for example, the Japanese-occupied city of Chongju was overrun by 1000 Korean irregulars. Then, in the last battle of 1592, a Korean force held off a samurai siege at Chinju Castle.

Chinju was defended by nearly 4000 Koreans armed with their own freshly-forged Korean arquebuses. The weapons, used in conjunction with mortar and cannon fire, gave the defenders an advantage against the attackers, who had

heavy stones and exploding bombs rained down upon them as they approached Chinju's walls. The samurai retreated, but returned with large bamboo shields and tall ladders to scale the walls.

Above: A 2010 re-enactment of Korean admiral Yi Sun-sin's funeral procession. Despite being outnumbered ten to one by the Japanese navy, Yi Sun-sin was undefeated at sea.

Left: Over 4000 Koreans held the defences at the castle of Chinju, raining down rocks, exploding bombs and boiling water on the Japanese soldiers scaling the walls.

Facing page: The second invasion of Korea in 1597 ended in stalemate for both sides. Over 180,000 Koreans lost their lives during the samurai invasions.

The defenders replied with long spears and pushed many samurai and their ladders from the walls. Samurai siege towers were hastily built in an attempt to provide cover for those scaling the walls, but the Koreans held their position. After three days of fighting the moat of Chinju was piled high with the samurai dead, and Korean reinforcements with fresh ammunition were attacking the Japanese back line. There was no choice but to retreat. The samurai defeat at Chinju was the beginning of the end of the Korean invasion.

The Long March Home
In P'yongyang, Yukinaga had met with Chinese envoys and claimed that Japan had no interest in China and wanted peace. A 50-day armistice was agreed to allow the Chinese Emperor to reflect. In reality, the Chinese used the time to assemble a 40,000-strong army under general Li Rusong. Yukinaga, on the other hand, had almost run out of rice. When the Chinese army finally reached P'yongyang, Yukinaga lost over 2000 men during the army's first assault. That night, under a bitterly cold sky, the Japanese abandoned P'yongyang and crossed the frozen Taedong River.

Above: Ulsan Castle was the setting for a Chinese and Korean siege in 1597 and 1598. On both occasions the samurai defenders successfully protected the castle.

Thus the retreat south began. Katō Kiyomasa was ordered back from his campaign in the northeast, which had been successful but also uneventful. Kiyomasa was reportedly furious when he learned his samurai counterparts, in particular Yukinaga, had failed in their mission. Yukinaga himself found that every Japanese outpost and stronghold had been abandoned as his army pushed south to Seoul. Rusong was ordered to chase the samurai invaders from the shores of Korea, but his own supply lines were now also being stretched to the limit. Seoul was one of the Japanese's last strongholds in Korea, and a full assault against its 20,000-strong samurai garrison would end in a bloodbath.

Instead, Rusong hoped the Korean guerillas would take care of the samurai on his behalf.

The same thought may have also occurred to the Japanese, who killed every Korean male in sight. Then they set fire to every field around Seoul, destroying all food sources for Rusong's cavalry. In this now bitter war between China and Japan, Korea was the biggest loser. There was widespread famine, disease and destruction, and reports of cannibalism among the last Korean inhabitants of Seoul.

In the end the samurai wanted to leave as much as the Koreans wanted to see them go. A terse meeting between the Chinese and Japanese in Seoul agreed that the samurai armies would be allowed to retreat south unhindered. As they marched, the samurai subjected the Koreans to gleeful degradation. But the samurai did not leave Korea altogether. Instead they kept some strongholds in the south as peace negotiations continued, with Yukinaga acting as Hideyoshi's main ambassador.

After many delays, a Chinese delegation visited Japan in 1596 with a letter for Hideyoshi from the Chinese Emperor. Incredibly, Hideyoshi had been kept in the dark about the full extent of the failure in Korea. Yukinaga had led him to believe that the letter would agree to all of his demands, issue an apology and offer to crown him as Emperor of China. Instead it referred to Hideyoshi as the 'King of Japan', rebuked him for his invasion and ordered that he dismantle all samurai strongholds in Korea and quit the country for good. It also warned that any Japanese vessel found in Chinese or Korean waters would be sunk without warning.

Hideyoshi's rage was so great that his head was said to smoke like fire and his body drip with sweat. He tore off the Chinese gifts of robes and a crown, which he believed to be some kind of coronation outfit, and ordered Yukinaga to commit sepukku on the spot. This order was rescinded, as Hideyoshi instead ordered a second invasion of Korea. This would not be as a prelude to the invasion of China, but simply to punish the Korean people themselves.

So it was that a new force of 140,000 samurai sailed back to Korea in 1597. But this time the Korean army was ready for them and, together with soldiers sent from China, it defeated the Japanese in 1598. The news of the second failure in Korea all but finished Hideyoshi. Later the same year the once-great general who had succeeded in uniting Japan died aged 62.

BATTLE OF SEKIGAHARA

Sekigahara is one of the most infamous and influential battles in samurai history. It was the day that two of the largest samurai forces ever assembled clashed in a chaotic melee filled with fog, rain, mud and confusion. Their prize was Japan itself, a country that had reverted to civil war following the death of its second great unifier Toyotomi Hideyoshi. Hideyoshi's heir was Hideyori, but his position as regent was under threat by Tokugawa Ieyasu, the most powerful daimyō in Japan.

Hideyori was directly represented by a samurai bureaucrat called Ishida Mitsunari. Mitsunari had won favour with Hideyoshi during the ill-fated invasion of Korea and now led the Eastern Army of 82,000 samurai. Leading the Western Army was of course Tokugawa Ieyasu, who commanded around

The Sekigahara Setting

Sekigahara was a narrow pass between the mountains of Mino province, north of Lake Biwa. Here, a crossroads intersected the valley, including the main Nakasendo road from the east. Another road led south to Ogaki and a third north to Lake Biwa. Rising above the valley was Mount Nangu and Mount Momokubari to the east, Mount Matsuo to the southwest, Mount Tengu to the west and Mount Sasao to the north. Ieyasu's Eastern Army would approach Sekigahara along the Nakasendo road. Mitsunari's divided force would be waiting for Ieyasu on Mount Nangu, Mount Matsuo and along the whole of the west side of the valley up to the slopes of Mount Sasao.

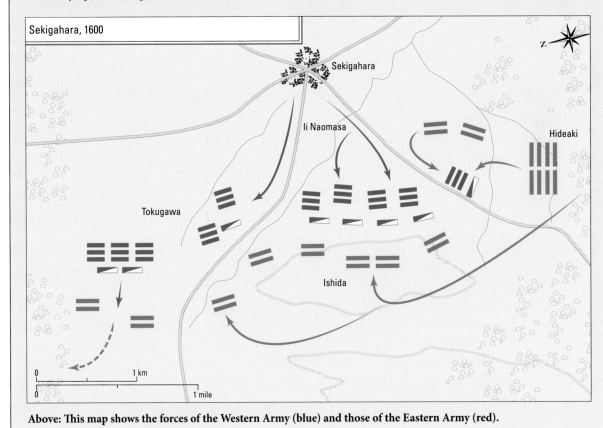

Above: This map shows the forces of the Western Army (blue) and those of the Eastern Army (red).

Sekigahara Armies

MAIN COMMANDERS
AND FORCES

Eastern Army:
  Tokugawa Ieyasu 30,000
  Il Naomasa 3600
  Honda Tadakatsu 500
  Kuroda Nagamasa 5400
  Asano Yukinaga 6510
  Hosokawa Tadaoki 5000
  Fukushima Masanori 6000

Western Army
  Ishida Mitsunari 4000
  Kobayakawa Hideaki 15,000
  Shimazu Yoshihiro 1500
  Mōri Hidemoto 15,000
  Ukita Hideie 17,000
  Konishi Yukinaga 4000
  Ōtani Yoshitsugu 3500
  Kikkawa Hiroie 3000

**Right: Eastern Army General
Honda Tadakatsu was famous for
adorning his helmets with deer
antlers. Here, the part
of Tadakatsu is played by a
re-enactor.**

88,000 samurai. Allies from the two armies clashed in a series of sieges and skirmishes in early 1600. But the combined forces of both sides would not meet in a pitched battle until 21 October at Sekigahara.

Mitsunari and his contingent of 4000 retainers arrived at Mount Matsuo at around 1am on 21 June. Here, Kobayakawa Hideaki and his 15,000 samurai had already secured a position with a clear view of the valley. After a short conference between the daimyō, it was agreed that Hideaki would lead a late charge into the Tokugawa troops below after Mitsunari gave him the signal. Mitsunari then rode to the foot of Mount Sasao to set up a command post. To his south were the Shimazu and various

Above: The 1600 Battle of Sekigahara was fought between two of the largest samurai armies ever assembled. Opportunism, treachery and chance were all played out on the battlefield.

Above: Hundreds of thousands of samurai assembled at Sekigahara, where they conducted a messy and muddy melee on the rain-soaked ground.

Facing page: After defeating the Western Army at Sekigahara, Tokugawa Ieyasu famously said: 'After victory, tighten the cords of your helmet.'

detachments totalling around 11,000 samurai. South of the Shimazu, at the foot of Mount Tengu, was Ukita Hideie's encamped force of around 17,000. On the east side of the valley, sitting atop Mount Nangu, was Mōri Hidemoto. Hidemoto overlooked the Nakasendo road along which Ieyasu's army would enter the valley in the morning. As with Kobayakawa Hideaki, Mōri Hidemoto would wait for Mitsunari's signal before charging down the mountain and into the fray.

Ieyasu's army began its approach into Sekigahara shortly after 2am on 21 June. The fog was so thick that the samurai complained they could not see the man in front of them, and the pass soon become a bog. In fact, the fog had been a blessing for Ieyasu, as it gave him absolute cover to enter the valley and take up position unseen and unhindered. Unbeknown to Ieyasu's front line, the enemy was only about 3.2km (2 miles) away when they stopped to build palisades and dig ditches in the saturated ground.

Cavalry Charge

At 8am the fog lifted and the armies' brightly coloured banners, flags and armour created a dazzling display for the generals looking down into

the valley. The Eastern Army's Ii Naomasa made the first charge, leading his brightly painted 'Red Devils' headfirst into Ukita Hideie's men. Naomasa's men charged with such force that that they actually broke through Hideie's lines and crashed into the first detachment of Shimazu samurai behind them. It became immediately clear that battle tactics and formations would have little bearing on the outcome at Sekigahara. Instead, the fighting would become a largely improvised affair, with mounted cavalry charges launched left, right and centre as lines of arqubusiers fired into the fray, adding smoke and explosions to the battlefield shouts and

screams. Pockets of hand-to-hand fighting broke out everywhere. Confused lines of samurai wading through the quagmire, hacking and slicing at the enemy as best they could.

It was difficult enough for the general of each division to keep track of his samurai, let alone the daimyō charged with commanding several divisions. The daimyō were a problem too. Both Mitsunari and Ieyasu's armies were being led by typically headstrong men, each with his own ideas about how the battle should go. Often these ideas were quite dissimilar from those of Mitsunari or Ieyasu.

One such daimyō was Shimazu Yoshihiro, a troublemaker from Kyūshū who seemed disinclined to enter the battle at all. When Mitsunari rode over to find out what had stalled Yoshihiro, the daimyō simply told him that each unit must be left free to fight when it thought best. This would have infuriated Mitsunari, but short of declaring war on his Shimazu allies all he could really do was wait and hope that Yoshihiro joined in at some point.

From the Eastern Army's side, Ieyasu was also looking for some decisive action on the battlefield. He ordered Kuroda Nagamasa to take 20,000 samurai and attack Mitsunari directly. By rendering the Western Army leaderless Ieyasu would bring a rapid victory. Mitsunari himself responded by pointing his heavy artillery at Nagamasa's approaching men, accomplishing little except to add to the noise, smoke and confusion in the valley below. Mitsunari's next move was to order Kobayakawa Hideaki to enter the battle. The signal fire was lit, but Hideaki, instead of giving the

order to attack, sat on his horse and gazed at the battle below.

Two of the Western Army commanders in the valley, Konishi Yukinaga and Ōtani Yoshitsugu, were appalled at Hideaki's inaction. Yukinaga sent a messenger to Hideaki demanding he do his duty, but the samurai leader remained impassively in his saddle. Yoshitsugu, a leper who was leading from the comfort of a palanquin, suspected the worst and ordered his samurai to ready themselves to train their arquebuses against a potential charge by their ally Hideaki. But Mitsunari and his commanders were not the only ones waiting for Hideaki's charge. Ieyasu himself had held a secret meeting with Hideaki days earlier, and had arranged for Hideaki to defect to his side. But now Hideaki simply sat immobile. Perhaps no-one will ever know what was going through Hideaki's mind that day. He had promised his sword to both armies and he now had the power to win the day for either side. Was he frightened, confused or just unwilling to commit his men to the messy chaos he saw in the valley below?

In the end, it was Ieyasu who took the biggest risk of the day to spur Hideaki's samurai into action. He sent a small contingent of arqubusiers to fire on Hideaki's position. Surprisingly, this move spurred Hideaki into life and ironically gave him the impetus to defect against his own side. Hideaki issued the command and his army of 15,000 samurai charged down the hill towards Yoshitsugu's line. But Yoshitsugu's men had been readied for this moment and trained their arquebuses at the oncoming

Reluctant Rebel?

At the time Hideyori was building Ieyasu's bell, there were rumours that he was amassing arms and men behind the thick walls of Ōsaka. This seems unlikely: Hideyori had sent back a quantity of gunpowder to an English factory in 1614 claiming he had no use for it. Instead, Ieyasu snapped up the consignment for himself at a cheap price. On the other hand, it was true that thousands of rōnin, disaffected Christians and various other malcontents were drifting into the confines of Ōsaka Castle. Many of these samurai were the remnants from the Battle of Sekigahara, masterless warriors with no banner to fight under but a fierce grudge against their persecutor, Tokugawa Ieyasu. Why Hideyori welcomed these men has never been clear. Was he building an army to wage war with Ieyasu, or simply preparing a defensive force to withstand the Taiko's inevitable attack?

Facing page: A memorial stone marks the site of the Battle of Sekigahara. Sekigahara ensured Ieyasu would become Shōgun and supreme unifier of Japan.

Ōsaka Defenders and Attackers

Main defending commanders and samurai:
  Toyotomi Hideyori 3000
  Sanada Yukimura 5000
  Gotō Mototsugu 3000
  Ōno Harunaga 5000
  Akashi Morishige 2000
  Kimura Shinenari 8000
  Mōri Katsunaga 5000
  Oda Yuraku 1300
  Chosokabe Mōrishige 5000

Main attacking commanders and samurai:
  Tokugawa Ieyasu 30,000
  Tokugawa Hidetada 20,000
  Date Masamune 10,000
  Uesugi Kagekatsu 5000
  Asano Nagakira 7000
  Honda Tadamasa 3000
  Li Naotaka 4000
  Maeda Toshitsune 12,000
  Mōri Hidenari 10,000

Facing page: Ōsaka Castle was a formidable complex that covered over 60,000 square metres of land. Today, the castle remains stand near the centre of Ōsaka City.

charge, picking off hundreds of Hideaki's samurai as they came. But their number was too great to hold off, and as the Yoshitsugu line was broken Ōtani Yoshitsugu committed seppuku in his palanquin.

Yoshihiro Retreats

Konishi Yukinaga and his men, also caught up in Hideaki's treacherous attack, fought to the death. But all seemed lost for the Western Army. Shimazu Yoshihiro, who had reluctantly joined the fighting, could see he was soon to be overrun by the Eastern Army. He decided to cut his losses and ordered a retreat. As the Shimazu samurai rode away from the battlefield, they called out to passers-by that the day was lost. As a result, large numbers of Western Army samurai waiting to bring up Mitsunari's rear deserted their posts before they had fired a shot.

There was only one hope left now for Mitsunari – Mōri Hidemoto. Hidemoto's force of 15,000 samurai sat waiting on Mount Nangu and below him a smaller force of 3000 samurai led by Kikkawa Hiroie. Both, in theory, were waiting to join the battle. Their combined force would have certainly swayed the battle in Mitsunari's favour but neither general gave the order to attack. It did not take long for Shimazu's message that the battle was lost to spread through the ranks and reach Mount Nangu. Hiroie and Hidemoto both gave the order to retreat.

By early afternoon the battle was over and Ieyasu was sitting on his stool surveying the large numbers of enemy samurai heads being brought to him. He had declined to wear his helmet all day, but now Ieyasu asked that it be brought to him, as he uttered

a saying which is still popular in Japan today: 'After victory, tighten the cords of your helmet.'

Mitsunari himself managed to escape from the battleground but was hunted down and beheaded some days later. Mitsunari's allies were either executed, invited to commit seppuku or stripped of their titles and domains. Those who had supported Ieyasu, and even those who had defected to him on the battlefield, were rewarded with land and titles.

Hideyori himself was not punished by death, but instead made to pay reparations, specifically by building a large statue of Buddha and a large bronze bell. The bell would give Ieyasu the justification to pursue Hideyori in the Siege of Ōsaka. So while Sekigahara was not the last battle of the samurai, it was the conflict that allowed Ieyasu to disable those daimyō who had fought against him and unite the country under his rule as Shōgun.

SIEGE OF ŌSAKA

The events at Ōsaka Castle from 1614 to 1615 mark the end of an important chapter in samurai history. It would be the last time two samurai armies met for a pitched battle on an open plain. It would also represent Tokugawa Ieyasu's final conflict before his death in 1615. His passing would signify the end of the Sengoku Jidai, or 'Age of the Warring States', which had begun in 1467. The Sengoku Jidai would be replaced by the Edo Period and 250 years of almost entirely peaceful rule under the Tokugawa Shōgunate. The Siege of Ōsaka completed the great unification of Japan and allowed for the ensuing period of peace. It was a campaign that the wily

Ōsaka Castle

Hideyoshi's Ōsaka Castle had been built to withstand a long siege by an attacking army armed with arquebuses and cannon. It was a massive complex with a keep at its heart, surrounded by thick stone walls, a horseshoe of wet moats as well as a dry moat. Surrounding these moats was the second part of the castle, a flat area containing samurai barracks, rice stores, an orchard, stables and other buildings. Protecting this area were thick high walls and another wet moat. Four fortified ramps, three protected by large gatehouses, linked the castle to the outside world. A last natural line of defence was created by the Temma, Yodo and Yamato Rivers to the north and the sea to the south.

Right: Toyotomi Hideyori's bronze bell with the two ideographs that caused so much offence to Ieyasu – 'Ie' and 'yasu' – highlighted in white.

Ieyasu had to win to secure his legacy. Ieyasu the Taiko, or retired Regent, had to use every ounce of his experience and cunning to win at Ōsaka. For protecting Ieyasu's quarry – Toyotomi Hideyori – was Ōsaka Castle, the strongest samurai fortress ever built. The Ōsaka campaign would be a classic samurai conflict, complete with sieges, skirmishes, deceit, betrayal and a brutal battlefield brawl at the end.

Ironically, Toyotomi Hideyori would probably have preferred to avoid a war with Ieyasu. Hideyori was born at the wrong time and to the wrong father, Toyotomi Hideyoshi. Hideyoshi had made Ieyasu swear a solemn oath on his deathbed that he would ensure Hideyori's position as Regent. No such thing happened. Instead Ieyasu had put down Hideyori's army, led by Ishida Mitsunari, at the 1600 Battle of Sekigahara.

The die was cast when Ieyasu ordered Hideyori to abandon his family home of Ōsaka Castle as part of a general redistribution of daimyō who had been hostile to him at Sekigahara. Hideyori said he would rather die than leave Ōsaka. Ieyasu agreed this might be best and set about assembling an army made up of samurai from his daimyō allies and the other, lesser daimyōs. Hideyori also sent out the call to daimyō who had at one time been loyal to his father. No large houses responded, but some of those who had fallen under Ieyasu's power after Sekigahara sent samurai to help. So began the Siege of Ōsaka, which was split into two sections – the 1614 Winter Campaign and the 1615 Summer Campaign.

The Winter Campaign

The Winter Campaign began with the mobilization of Ieyasu's army from Edo and the strengthening of defences at Ōsaka Castle. The weakest point of the castle, if there was one, was along its south-facing

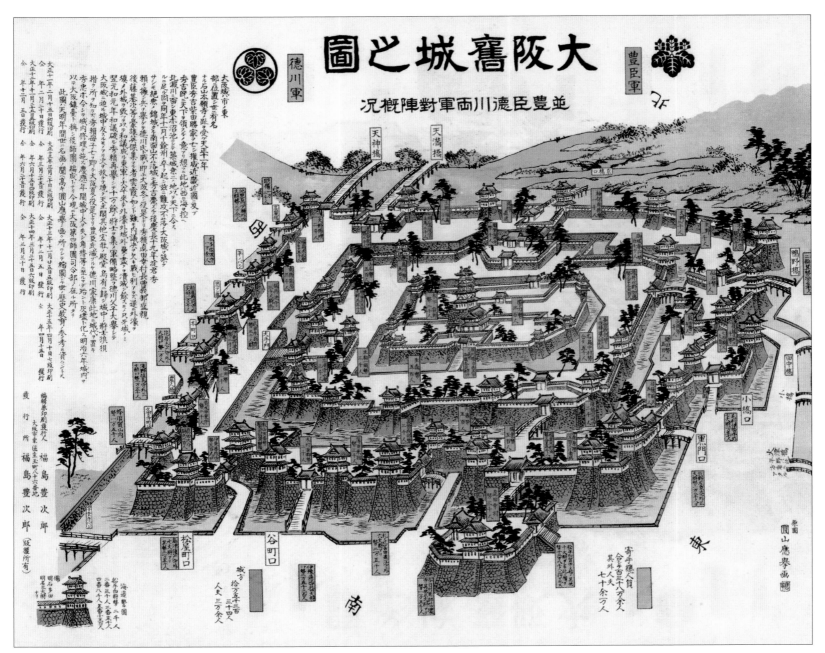

Left: Ōsaka Castle protected its inner keep with dry and wet moats, a series of thick stone walls and fortified ramps and gatehouses.

side. This was the only flat, dry land where an army could encamp and dig itself in, and in anticipation of this Sanada Yukimura built a large outer moat, a barbican, a wall and palisades on the south plain. Fortifications complete, Hideyori's 60,000-strong army prepared for the arrival of Ieyasu.

Ieyasu's full force was around 180,000-strong by the time it reached Ōsaka. Ieyasu quickly wiped out any resistance from the outposts around the castle and then encamped, as expected, in the area south of the castle. From this vantage point, a series of raids began on Yukimura's barbican in January 1615. But three divisions of Ieyasu's samurai were quickly beaten back, mainly by arquebus-carrying ashigaru positioned along the walls. It soon became obvious to Ieyasu that an all-out assault on the castle walls would not work. A siege would have to be staged.

Ieyasu probably had some idea of the difficulty of besieging Ōsaka Castle before he began. The advantage lay with the defenders, who had access to a well inside the castle walls and enough rice to feed the whole army for several years. The attackers, by comparison, would be left outside to suffer the bitter cold of the winter months. Ieyasu kept up the pretence of making inroads by bombarding the castle with cannon and trying to undermine its walls. Neither tactic was successful and it was clear that Ōsaka Castle could withstand its attackers. Stalemate seemed imminent. A siege could not continue indefinitely, and Ieyasu was losing face. How long before unsatisfied daimyō began marching their armies home, or worse, defected to Hideyori?

Diplomatic Strategies

Ieyasu opted for a more political route. First he tried to bribe Sanada Yukimura from the castle walls. When this failed he attempted the less obvious route with Hideyori's mother, Yodogimi. To persuade Yodogimi he bombarded the royal quarters around the clock for three days. Only one or two cannonballs actually hit the walls, but the psychological damage was huge. A desperate Yodogimi pleaded with her son to agree to Ieyasu's terms, and eventually Hideyori gave in.

The peace treaty gave the Ōsaka rōnin a pardon and allowed Hideyori to live wherever he pleased. In return, Hideyori would have to swear not to rebel against Ieyasu again. Ieyasu then announced there 'would be no more wars', a catchphrase that was to re-emerge several times during later times. This might have sounded reasonable, but most correctly regarded the document and the treaty to be a farce. Both Sekigahara and the winter siege had presented a real threat to Ieyasu's domination of Japan. After 60 years of unification, Ieyasu was not going to stumble at the last post. Hideyori would have to go. It was just a matter of when.

After the signing of the peace treaty on 22 January, Ieyasu's army began pulling down Ōsaka's outer wall and using the material to fill in the castle moat. There were protests from the castle, but these were quickly silenced by the 'no more wars' argument. After all, if there were to be no more wars, why did Hideyori need a moat? By the time the Tokugawa packed up their sledgehammers Ōsaka Castle had been reduced to one moat and one

outer wall. All Ieyasu now needed was an excuse, however flimsy, to march his army back to Ōsaka, storm the castle and kill the Toyotomi leader he had sworn to serve, protect and obey.

The Summer Campaign

The pretext arrived in the summer of 1615, when rumours circulated that Hideyori was digging out his moat and building new defences. Then reports reached Ieyasu that thousands of rōnin and Christian samurai were flocking to Ōsaka Castle. The size of Hideyori's army would reach 120,000 by the time Ieyasu arrived back in Ōsaka at the head of his own 250,000-strong army. But this time there would no long and protracted siege. Instead both armies met in a pitched battle on the plain of Tennoji, near Ōsaka Castle.

The size of the two armies showed just how far samurai warfare had come since the early medieval period. Now there were no challenges or mounted duels to signal the start of combat. Instead, lines of ashigaru marched towards each other carrying arquebuses and long lances. Even the horses had been left far behind the army ranks at Ieyasu's insistence. This was no longer clan warfare, where heroism and individual prowess could help win the day. This was modern warfare, fought between two armies who battled and killed each other anonymously, without a care for rank or family lineage.

The Ōsaka rōnin showed their lack of discipline and disregard for the ancient rules of samurai warfare. Although under the command of veteran Mōri Katsunaga, a couple of the rōnin fired their

Below: One of Tokugawa Ieyasu's siege
tactics at Ōsaka Castle was to pile bundles
of burning bamboo at the foot of the
fortress walls.

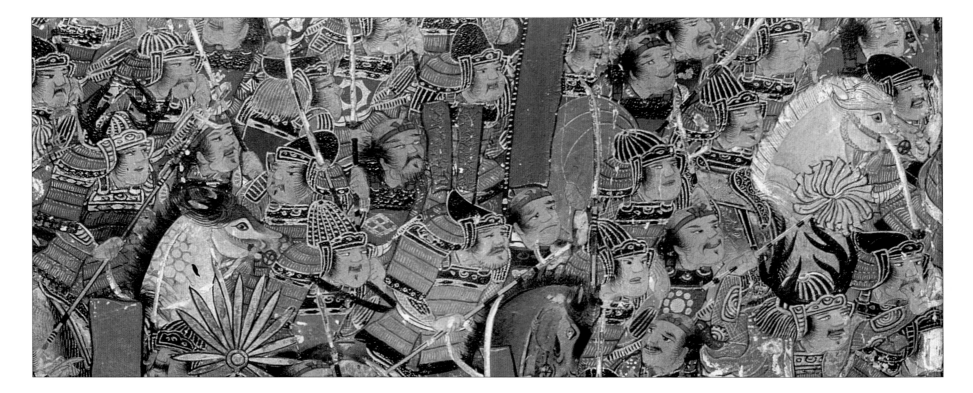

Above: A folding screen depicts Ieyasu's 250,000-strong army meeting Hideyori's 120,000-strong army on the plain of Tennōji, near Ōsaka Castle.

Facing page: The Battle of Tennōji, 3 June 1615. By the end of the day, Hideyori had lost the battle, Ōsaka Castle, and his life.

arquebuses prematurely at the enemy line opposite them, and the rest of the rōnin followed. Rather than stop the volley, Katsunaga called for the rōnin to charge at the Tokugawa force. This they did successfully, fully overwhelming the first lines of the enemy. Sanada Yukimura then led his men into the left flank of the Tokugawa army. As the Ōsaka rōnin also started breaking through to the left flank, the Tokugawa became disorientated trying to fight on two fronts. The battle fell into chaotic hand-to-hand fighting, where orders meant little amid the desperate hacking and killing. The day looked to be turning towards Hideyori's men, and

Ieyasu himself rode into the fray to try and help the men of his left flank. The Toyotomi plan was for Hideyori to ride out from the castle with a second army of rōnin to bolster numbers on the plain, but he was nowhere to be seen. Instead, events were turning Ieyasu's way, as Honda Tadamasa led his force of several thousand samurai to reinforce the failing Tokugawa left flank. As the battle tilted in the Tokugawa's favour, Sanada Yukimura was beheaded by an enemy warrior.

It was at this point that Hideyori rode out from Ōsaka Castle and stopped to observe the fracas. The plan was for him to join battle and rally his

men. But instead he turned around and led his men back inside. The Ōsaka army on the battlefield was also being pushed back, and soon retreated inside the castle walls to join Hideyori. But this time the Tokugawa forces were not going to be stopped. They scaled the castle walls and the battle turned into a ferocious melee of one-to-one combat.

Usurpers Beheaded

Hideyori managed to escape to the castle keep, but the rest of the fortress was quickly overrun by the Tokugawa. Now the process of putting Ōsaka Castle to the sword began in earnest. Civilians as well as Ōsaka samurai were butchered and the Tokugawa cannon fired relentlessly at the residential buildings inside the castle keep. Here, as the flames rose around his fallen fortress, Hideyori and Yodogimi committed seppuku. The next day, to make sure no Toyotomi heir would ever challenge the rule of the Tokugawa, Hideyori's eight-year-old son was beheaded. Large numbers of the Ōsaka samurai met the same fate, and their heads were put on display to show the world what happened to usurpers under the Tokugawa Shōgunate. The war had been won and Ieyasu was triumphant. His descendants would rule Japan for the next 250 years, a period of peace that ironically would make the samurai all but redundant. The Siege of Ōsaka would be remembered, but unlike the Gempei War and the samurai heroes of early Japan, its story would never be painted in romantic colours. Those times, along with any pretence of honour or chivalry in warfare, had passed.

Left: A memorial stone marks the place of Hideyori's death. Hideyori and his mother, Yodogimi, both committed seppuku as Ōsaka Castle burned around them.

Facing page: Tokugawa Ieyasu examines Kimura Shigenari's head following the Battle of Tennōji. Ieyasu was said to have had the hair on Shigenari's head trimmed out of respect.

Weapons and Armour

'To master the virtue of the long sword is to govern the world and oneself, thus the long sword is the basis of strategy. The principle is "strategy by means of the long sword". If he attains the virtue of the long sword, one man can beat ten men. Just as one man can beat ten, so a hundred men can beat a thousand, and a thousand can beat ten thousand. In my strategy, one man is the same as ten thousand, so this strategy is the complete warrior's craft.'

Miyamoto Musashi, *Go Rin No Sho*

SWORDS

The sword was the samurai's primary weapon and a prized possession that would only leave his side upon death. But it was more than just an instrument of war. The sword, described as 'the soul of the samurai', was believed to be a spiritual extension of the warrior himself. It was also a symbol of the ethos of the Way of the Warrior, a desire for balance, harmony and perfection. It took expert swordsmiths months to create a new sword and only the best blades would pass muster. The perfection required in the sword's manufacture was matched by the samurai's lifelong quest for perfection in the art of sword-fighting. Together, a samurai and his sword were an inseparable unit. This was even made law in 1588, when Toyotomi

Facing page: The samurai's sword was his prized possession that he would only part with in death. Here, twelfth century Emperor Toba forges himself a new sword.

Right: Miyamoto Musashi has his fortune told. He is often considered the greatest samurai who ever lived. In combat, he was as effective with a wooden bokken as a steel katana.

Right: Each samurai warrior carried two swords in his belt sash. By the mid-sixteenth century these were most commonly the short wakizashi and the long katana.

Hideyoshi decreed that only samurai could carry swords. From then on, the sword acted as the samurai's identity badge, setting him above and apart from other citizens as a member of the ruling class of Japan.

The earliest samurai swords were copies of the Chinese model, a long, straight sword used for stabbing. By the eighth century Japanese swordsmiths had improved upon the design by introducing a gentle curve, which changed the action of the sword from a thrusting to a cutting weapon. By the mid sixteenth century, the katana, as it was called, was considered the ultimate sword, the result of centuries of development in sword making. A samurai carried his katana in his belt sash, alongside a shorter, matching companion sword, most popularly the wakizashi. A matching set of a katana and a wakizashi were known as a daishō. The wakizashi, used to commit seppuku, never left a samurai's belt even in important conferences when his katana was laid to one side.

The katana was worn with its cutting edge upwards, to enable the extraction of the blade from its scabbard and into an enemy in one stroke. Today a katana is still considered one of the best cutting blades in the world, easily slicing through flesh and bone. Once created, a katana was tested out by cutting through the limbs of prisoners or, in times of peace, cadavers. Often corpses were piled one on

Anatomy of a Sword

Once the samurai blade had finished being polished it was mounted with a handle, hand-guard, scabbard and collar. Each of these fittings was completed by a specialist artisan before the sword was presented to its new owner.

TSUBA (HAND-GUARD)

The job of the disc-shaped tsuba was to prevent the warrior's hand slipping onto his own blade, and to block the blades of others. Early tsuba were made of wrought iron, but solid tsuba made of softer metals became popular from the Edo Period. These highly decorated tsuba often depicted scenes from nature or samurai heroes of the past.

TSUKA (HANDLE)

First a wooden handle was fitted to the bottom of a samurai blade and covered in ray skin. Silk or thread was then wrapped around the handle to provide grip. The inner diamond gaps left between the thread covering were designed according to the artisan's particular style.

HABAKI (COLLAR)

This wedge-shaped collar stopped the katana from falling out of the saya and helped keep the fittings in place.

SAYA (SCABBARD)

Saya were made of wood and usually lacquered black. Later Edo models often featured elaborate gold leaf designs. A loophole was included at the top of the Saya for a cord to be added, and sometimes a slot for a small utility knife known as a kogatana.

SAEGO (CORD)

The saego was designed to tie the saya to the warrior's belt sash to keep it in place. Saego came in a variety of colours and designs representing the wearer's clan and sometimes his status or age.

Above: The genius of the katana was its bimetallic makeup. A high-carbon steel shell for cutting was wrapped around a lower-carbon body which absorbed shock.

top of another on a bed of sand to see how many a katana could cut through in one slice. A good blade could cut through three bodies and an exceptional one could get through seven.

The katana derived its power from a hard cutting edge and a strong broad back. All samurai swords were two-handed weapons, and as such needed to act as a shield as well as a blade. To create a sword with a sharp cutting blade that could also absorb shock required two types of steel – a hard, high-carbon shell wrapped around a softer, lower-carbon body. This bi-metallic makeup was the genius of the samurai sword, the creation of which was considered a sacred art that took years of dedicated training to perfect. It took expert swordsmiths several months to complete a samurai sword. While they made it the swordsmiths would dress in white ceremonial clothes, perform Shinto rituals and forgo worldly pleasures.

Just to create the steel for a sword was an arduous process. It took 10 men more than three days to smelt the carbon-rich steel pieces that would be forged into a blade. To make the steel, iron sand was poured into a 1000-degree charcoal-fed furnace called a tatara. Then, over a pivotal 72-hour-period the sand would form into pieces of crude, high-carbon steel known as tamahagane. Once cooled,

the best tamahagane pieces were chosen for the forging process.

A swordsmith would craft the steel into a new samurai blade over several weeks. His team would include smiths to forge the blade's shape, assistant smiths to fold the metal with hammers, a polisher, a blade expert and sheath and hilt artisans. To create the sword, the tamahagane pieces were heated in a 1300-degree furnace and then folded up to 30 times through hammering to weld the steel together and distribute its carbon content evenly. A bar of lower-carbon steel was then inserted into a U-shaped piece of high-carbon steel, and hammered together to form the blade's soft interior and hard shell.

Once the blade had been hammered into the correct shape, around 60–80cm (23–31in) long, it was covered in a clay paste, which was then removed along the cutting edge. The blade was then reheated in the furnace and plunged into cold water. The result was a final hardening of the sword's cutting edge. If the blade had survived this process without cracking – and not all did – it spent several days being polished. This meant being rubbed with many different grades of increasingly fine stone, until the well-known wavy line that separates the hardened and unhardened steel showed, and the blade was brought to a dazzling finish.

Left: Sword polishing was one part of a sword's creation and was considered a sacred art. Different gradients of sharpening stone were used in the polishing.

The Art of Swordsmanship

From the moment a young samurai was given his first katana, his life would be dedicated to learning the art of swordsmanship. There was a lot to learn, starting with how to grasp the sword correctly with both hands and the different methods of drawing it from the scabbard. There was also sword etiquette, an all-important set of social rules that no samurai could afford to ignore. The most serious of these concerned 'scabbards hitting', which, as the samurai sword was considered an extension of the samurai himself, was tantamount to slapping the owner in the face. To preserve his honour, the aggrieved party would be expected to retaliate by drawing his sword and attacking the offending party. A famous example of a scabbards hitting incident is described below:

'Two officers belonging to the Emperor's staff met upon the imperial staircase; their swords happened to entangle, and words arose. Said one to the other, coolly, "It is only an accident, and at best it is only a quarrel between the two swords." "We shall see about that," cried the other, excitedly; and with these words he drew his weapon and plunged it into his breast. The other, impatient to obtain the same advantage, hurried away upon some errand of service which he was slowly performing, and instantly returned to his antagonist, who was

BASIC DRAW

Samurai would spend hours training in the 16 varieties of cut used with a katana. A smooth action to release the katana from its scabbard and into a cut was of paramount importance.

OVERHEAD CUT

The katana was a weapon used for slashing and cutting rather than stabbing. Most of the varieties of cut used by the samurai therefore featured a downwards stroke.

A

B

C

D

A

B

C

D

SIDEWAYS SWING

A sideways stroke was an essential cut that needed to be mastered by every samurai. Often, it would be used to behead an enemy warrior in battle.

A

B

C

D

GUARD POSTURE

According to master swordsman Minamoto Musashi, a samurai's stance was all important: 'It is necessary to maintain the combat stance in everyday life and to make your everyday stance your combat stance.'

Above and facing page: Master swordsman Miyamoto Musashi often fought according to Nitōjutsu, or the 'two sword' method. Musashi argued that Nitōjutsu was the logical method for all samurai: 'Let it suffice to say that in our land, whatever the reason, a warrior carries two swords at his belt. It is the way of the warrior.'

already at the point of death. On inquiring if he was still alive, and being informed of the fact, he also plunged his sword into his own body, exclaiming, "You should not have had the start of me if you had not found me engaged in the service of the Prince. I die contented, however, since I have had the glory of convincing you that my sword is as good as yours."

The Field of Honor, Benjamin C. Truman, 1884.

As part of their training samurai would become expert in the 16 varieties of cut, most of which used a downwards stroke. Young samurai practised their cuts on the bodies of criminals, either dead or alive, so they could experience slicing human flesh. Hours could be devoted to learning one move. Iaijutsu,

for example, was a single, smooth action that pulled the katana from its scabbard, struck down the opponent, wiped the blade clean of blood and returned the sword to its sheath.

The Book of Five Rings

As well as learning basic sword-fighting methods, samurai were also expected to study the techniques of others. One of the greatest masters of the samurai sword was Miyamoto Musashi, who recorded his accomplishments in *Go Rin No Sho*, 'The Book of Five Rings', a manual on sword-fighting strategy. Born in 1584, Musashi was an eccentric who seldom washed, was always late for duels and often preferred to fight with a wooden bokken rather than a katana. His skill with the

katana, however, meant that he could split a grain of rice on a man's forehead without drawing blood. At 15 years of age, Musashi went on a sword-fighting pilgrimage through the country and had soon dispatched more warriors in duels than any other samurai in the history of Japan. But after killing samurai master Sasaki Kojirō in a duel using the oar from a boat, Musashi gave up duelling altogether and spent the rest of his life considering the principles of sword fighting.

'When I reached 30 I looked back on my past,' he said. 'The previous victories were not due to my having mastered strategy. Perhaps it was natural ability, or the order of heaven or that other schools' strategy was inferior. After that I studied morning and evening searching for the principle, and came

to realize the "Way of Strategy" when I was 50.' When he was 60, Musashi retired to live in a cave and write *Go Rin No Sho*. He died in 1645, and was found sitting bolt upright with his wakizashi at the ready in his belt.

Musashi Cuts and Strokes

Miyamoto Musashi favoured a type of swordplay called Nitōjutsu, or the 'two sword' method. In *Go Rin No Sho* Musashi suggests: 'It is not difficult to wield a sword in one hand; the way to learn this is to train with two long swords, one in each hand. It will seem difficult at first, but everything is difficult at first.' Musashi also gave instruction about specific cuts and moves to be used in combat. The following examples are taken from *Go Rin No Sho*:

Right: A samurai swordsman is shown here alongside a naginata. The naginata was the first great battlefield leveller, designed to bring down a samurai on horseback.

'To Hit the Enemy in One Timing'

'In One Timing' means when you have closed with the enemy to hit him as quickly and directly as possible, without moving your body or settling your spirit, while you see that he is still undecided. The timing of hitting before the enemy decides to withdraw, break or hit, is this 'In One Timing'.

'Continuous Cut'

When you attack and the enemy also attacks, and your swords spring together, in one action cut his head, hands and legs. When you cut several places with one sweep of the long sword, it is the 'Continuous Cut'. You must practise this cut; it is often used. With detailed practice you should be able to understand it.

'Cut and Slash'

To cut and to slash are two different things. Cutting, whatever form of cutting it is, is decisive, with a resolute spirit. Slashing is nothing more than touching the enemy. Even if you slash strongly, and even if the enemy dies instantly, it is slashing. When you cut, your spirit is resolved. You must appreciate this. If you first slash the enemy's hands or legs, you must then cut strongly. Slashing is in spirit the same as touching. When you realize this, they become indistinguishable. Learn this well.

Left: The bow was the samurai's traditional weapon, originally fired from horseback. Bows were also used by nobles and courtiers in hunting and archery contests.

'Glue and Lacquer Emulsion Body'
The spirit of 'Glue and Lacquer Emulsion Body' is to stick to the enemy and not separate from him. When you approach the enemy, stick firmly with your head, body and legs. People tend to advance their head and legs quickly, but their body lags behind. You should stick firmly so that there is not the slightest gap between the enemy's body and your body. You must consider this carefully.

'To Scold "Tut-TUT!"'
Scold means that, when the enemy tries to counter-cut as you attack, you counter-cut again from below as if thrusting at him, trying to hold him down. With very quick timing you cut, scolding the enemy. Thrust up, 'Tut!', and cut 'TUT!' This timing is encountered time and time again in exchange of blows. The way to scold 'Tut-TUT' is to time the cut simultaneously with raising your long sword as if to thrust the enemy. You must learn this through repetitive practice.

Miyamoto Musashi, *Go Rin No Sho*

SECONDARY WEAPONS
The Bow
'The bow is tactically strong at the commencement of battle, especially battles on a moor, as it is possible to shoot quickly from among the spearmen. However, it is unsatisfactory in sieges,

Below: Samurai bows employed an off-centre grip so they could be fired accurately from horseback. This convention remained in place for archers firing from the ground.

Below: Samurai bows employed an off-centre grip so they could be fired accurately from horseback. This convention remained in place for archers firing from the ground.

or when the enemy is more than forty yards away. For this reason there are nowadays few traditional schools of archery. There is little use nowadays for this skill.'

Miyamoto Musashi, *Go Rin No Sho*

The main samurai weapons used in conjunction with the sword were the bow, naginata, spear and arquebus. During Japan's early Heian Period (794–967), the bow rather than the sword was a samurai's main weapon and used primarily in mounted duels.

Samurai bows were made from bamboo strips and wood, glued together, wrapped with rattan and then lacquered. This made the bow strong, rigid and tremendously hard to draw, which an archer would do using his thumb and forefinger. A further quirk was the bow's off-centre grip, which meant the arrow was shot from the bow around one third of the way up its shaft. This adaptation was to make it possible for a samurai to shoot from horseback, and allowed the bow to keep a length of 2–2.7m (6ft 6in–8ft 10in) without being shortened. Bowstrings were made from plant fibre and covered with wax.

Archery Skills

It took years to train an archer to fire a bow with the required power and precision for war, and a warrior's accomplishments with a bow were therefore often celebrated. One notable example is Minamoto Tametomo, a famous hero from the Gempei War renowned for his skills. After being captured by the enemy, Tametomo managed to escape punishment by decapitation but instead had the sinew on his bow arm severed. Despite this enforced disability, Tametomo was later reported to sink a boatload of enemy by firing an arrow though the vessel's hull from the shore.

However, the bow's position as the mainstay of the samurai's arsenal would not last. For one thing, it was extraordinarily difficult to wield a bow and ride a horse at the same time, and mounted warriors needed an assistant on hand to help them. This did not fit with the Sengoku Jidai's stripped-down approach to warfare and its more efficient forms of weaponry. Mounted warriors replaced their bows with spears, and bows were relegated to lines of ashigaru. These lines would usually fire volleys at the start of a battle as the other side launched charges against them. From the mid-sixteenth century, arquebuses would also be used in this position and in time they would outnumber and overtake the bow and arrow.

Yajiri

Arrow shafts were made of bamboo and fletched with sea eagle, hawk or pheasant feathers. Arrowheads, or yajiri, were made from the same tamahagane steel used for samurai swords. There were hundreds of different yajiri styles and shapes, all with a particular function. During the Heian Period (794–1185), the first arrow fired in a

Left: Minamoto Yoshitsune was a famous figure of the Gempei War. He is pictured armed with a bow and wearing typical twelfth century armour.

battle would be the kabura-ya, a wooden top that hummed as it sailed through the air to draw the attention of the gods to the battlefield bravery that was to follow. The karimata arrowhead constructed in a 'V' shape was supposedly designed to disrobe a warrior by cutting the cords that held his armour in place. The following examples were some of the most commonly used yajiri.

Naginata and Yari

'The naginata is inferior to the yari on the battlefield. With the yari you can take the initiative; the naginata is defensive. In the hands of one of two men of equal ability, the spear gives a little extra strength. Yari and naginata both have their uses, but neither is very beneficial in confined spaces. They cannot be used for taking a prisoner. They are essentially weapons for the field.'

Miyamoto Musashi, *Go Rin No Sho*

The naginata was a weapon that first featured heavily in samurai warfare of the twelfth century. It was a particular long-term favourite of the sohei warrior monks, who often played a starring role during the Gempei War. One such sohei was Gochiin-no-Tajima, whose skill with the naginata at the 1180 Battle of the Uji Bridge was recounted in the epic Genpei War chronicle, the *Heike Monogatari*:

Common Yajiri

TOGARI-YA (pointed)
The main battle arrow in an archer's quiver.

YANAGI-BA (willow leaf)
Used predominantly from the mid-sixteenth century, this willow-leaf-shaped arrow featured designs such as hearts, cherry blossom or the clan's mon (its emblem).

KABURA-YA (whistling arrows)
These 'humming bulb' arrows were used at the start of combat to signal troops, invite the attention of the gods and inspire terror in the hearts of the enemy.

KARIMATA (rope cutter)
The karimata came in a variety of sizes and was used to cut lacing and ropes, hunt game and disable horses legs.

WATAKUSHI (barbed)
Designed to inflict terrible wounds, the watakusi measured between two and 15cm (0.7–5.9in) and featured single or double barbs.

Above: Togari-ya (pointed); Karimata (rope cutter)

'Gochiin-no-Tajima, throwing away the sheath of his long naginata, strode forth alone on to the bridge, whereupon the Heike straightaway shot at him fast and furious. Tajima, not at all perturbed, ducking to avoid the higher ones and leaping up over those that flew low, cut through those that flew straight with his whirring naginata, so that even the enemy looked on in admiration. Thus it was that he was dubbed "Tajima the arrow cutter."'

The *Heike Monogatari*
translated by A. L. Sadler, 1918

The popularity of the naginata and another polearm, the yari spear, greatly increased after the failed thirteenth-century Mongol invasion of Japan. Battles against other samurai were one thing, but when confronted by an enemy who cared little for the ritual of mounted duels or notions of honour in warfare, Japanese warriors were forced to rethink their approach. It was obvious that the least efficient

Below: The naginata typically featured a 30–60 cm (12–23 inch) long, curved blade attached to a long shaft. The blade was forged in the same way as a katana.

Right: This nineteenth century woodblock print depicts a rōnin deflecting arrows with his naginata. Rōnin were masterless samurai who often worked as swords for hire.

Yari

Yari from the mid-sixteenth century had a lacquered, hardwood shaft between 4m and 6.5m (13ft 1in–21ft 4in) long. A typical yari blade was up to 1m (3ft 3in) long and made of the same tamahagane steel as a samurai sword. Some of the most popular types of yari are listed below.

JUMONJI YARI
A cross-shaped yari also called a magari yari, with one straight central blade and two slightly curved flanking blades.

YAJIRI NARI YARI
A spade-shaped yari featuring two central holes.

TSUKI NARI YARI
A yari with a crescent-shaped blade for slashing and hooking.

SASAHO YARI
A yari with a broad, bamboo-shaped blade.

SANKAKU YARI
A yari without a cutting edge, but instead a strong point for penetrating armour.

Left: Two samurai grapple with a yari – a polearm with a straight blade around one metre long. Yaris would gradually replace naginatas on the battlefield.

Facing page: Replica arquebuses are fired during a battle re-enactment. Here, the blue burning fuse is used to ignite the charge and fire the arquebus.

way of bringing down an archer on horseback was by using another archer on horseback. Instead, it was simpler for several ashigaru armed with naginatas to attack a rider collectively. The naginata, with its 30–60 cm (12–23.6in) curved blade attached to a long shaft, was the perfect weapon for unhorsing a warrior.

It was also simpler for a mounted warrior to abandon his bow altogether in favour of a yari. The yari was constructed from a straight blade that sharpened to an end point. This made it a versatile weapon that could be used by a horseman in the fashion of a lance from medieval Europe, but also allowed for the slashing action of a naginata. From the time of the Sengoku Jidai, lines of ashigaru carrying naginatas and yaris would be a mainstay of a daimyō's army. These lines would launch a charge at the enemy lines, often after a volley of arrows or fire by front lines of arquebus-armed ashigaru and ashigaru archers.

Both Oda Nobunaga and Toyotomi Hideyoshi were great advocates of the yari, with samurai of the Oda clan carrying yari over 6m (19ft) long. Seven of Hideyoshi's generals who outdid themselves with yari at the 1583 Battle of

Anatomy of an Arquebus

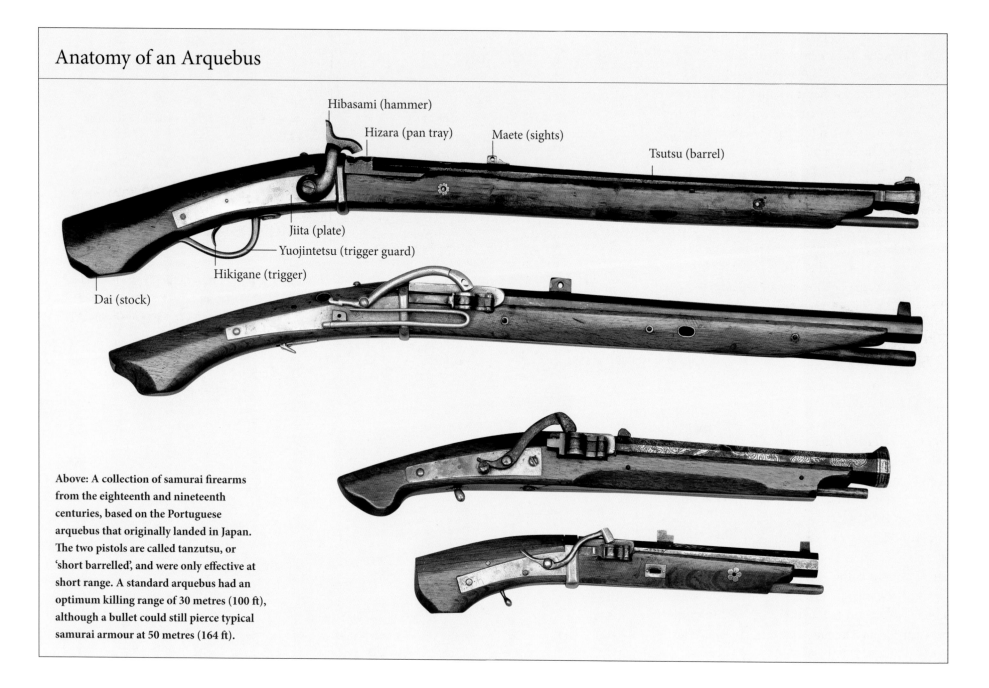

Hibasami (hammer)

Hizara (pan tray)

Maete (sights)

Tsutsu (barrel)

Jiita (plate)

Yuojintetsu (trigger guard)

Hikigane (trigger)

Dai (stock)

Above: A collection of samurai firearms from the eighteenth and nineteenth centuries, based on the Portuguese arquebus that originally landed in Japan. The two pistols are called tanzutsu, or 'short barrelled', and were only effective at short range. A standard arquebus had an optimum killing range of 30 metres (100 ft), although a bullet could still pierce typical samurai armour at 50 metres (164 ft).

Shizugadake became famously known as the 'Seven Famous Spearmen of Shizugatake'. One of these samurai was Katō Kiyomasa whose skill with the yari was further demonstrated during the Korean invasion of 1592. Here, Kiyomasa famously speared a tiger while subduing the inhabitants of the country's north east.

By the time of the 1600 Battle of Sekigahara, the yari had overtaken the naginata as the polearm of choice, and the weapon was used extensively by Tokugawa Ieyasu's front lines. It was also used to great effect during the Siege of Ōsaka's Battle of Tennoji, the last pitched battle of the samurai. Following Ieyasu's demise and the onset of the Edo Period, yari would still be manufactured but more as a ceremonial object than a practical weapon of war. Antique naginata blades were also often remounted as wakizashi daggers at this time.

THE ARQUEBUS

'From inside fortifications, the gun has no equal among weapons. It is the supreme weapon on the field before the ranks clash, but once swords are crossed the gun becomes useless.'

Miyamoto Musashi, *Go Rin No Sho*

The arquebus was the late, great breakthrough in the samurai arsenal that ensured success and carnage on the battlefield in equal measures. There was little contest between a samurai bow and an arquebus. The bow had an optimum killing range of between 30 and 50m (98–164ft), and the arquebus between 50 and 200m (98–656ft). The arquebus's

Miscellaneous Samurai Weapons

KANABŌ
A heavy club made of solid wood or iron with studs or spikes at one end. A kanabo was between 15cm (6in) and 2m (6ft 7in) long and was commonly used to break bones and the legs of horses.

HACHIWARA
Known as 'skull breaker', the hachiwara was a long, thin dagger used for penetrating weak points of an opponent's armour or helmet.

ONO
A war axe or hatchet, favoured by the sohei warrior monks.

OTSUCHI
A large war hammer used in battle and to break down gates.

SODEGARAMI
Known as the 'sleeve entangler', the sodegarami was a 2m- (6ft 7in-) long polearm with barbs and spikes used as a man-catcher.

TESSEN
A war fan made of iron plates that could be used to throw, fend off arrows and attack enemies. Other war fans included the gunbai and the gunsen.

Above: War fans were commonly used by generals as signalling devices, but they also doubled as weapons.

Left: A stylized image of the 1877 defeat of Saigō Takamori, often considered 'the last samurai'. Takamori's swords were no match for modern rifles and Gatling guns.

adoption into the ranks of Oda Nobunaga's army won the daimyō a pivotal victory at the 1575 Battle of Nagashino and guaranteed his place as the first great unifier of Japan. His secret had been to use the clumsy and slow-to-reload firearm in a rotating front line so that a sustained volley could be maintained. His methods would be continued by his successors, Hideyoshi and Ieyasu, who used the weapon to secure their domination over all other Japanese daimyō.

Naval Firepower

While arquebus technology was extremely popular among samurai warriors, the development of cannon did not have the same reputation. Cannons were found harder to replicate than arquebuses and those imported from Europe were considered the most effective. Japanese cannons, by comparison, were strange confections often consisting of a large barrel tied on to a cart, or built into a box-like wooden stock. While samurai cannons used in the field of battle were generally considered ineffective noise-makers, they were put to better use at sea, notably in Oda Nobunaga's 1573 Siege of Nagashima. Here, cannons were crucial, destroying the castle walls and bringing an end to the siege. Tokugawa Ieyasu also famously trained his cannons on the residential castle buildings at the 1614–15

Siege of Ōsaka, but again this was more effective in straining the nerves of the inhabitants than bringing down walls.

While swordsmiths struggled with the manufacture of cannons, it did not take them long to accurately reproduce arquebuses in large numbers following the weapon's 1543 arrival in Japan. The barrels were constructed by wrapping a long, hot steel plate around a rod that was then removed. The stock was made of wood and the lock mechanism and decorative inlays of brass. The arquebus employed the matchlock system, which required the user to light a long fuse that fell into a touchhole to spark the charge. This gave the user time to take aim before the weapon fired, unlike earlier versions that required a live match to be dropped into the touchhole. Despite this small advance, an arquebus was notoriously difficult to light in the wind or rain, and its gunpowder was easily made damp and ineffective.

While the arquebus played a large role in bringing about the unification of Japan and the 250 years of peace that followed, its history is short compared with that of the samurai warrior. The arquebus was used in warfare for only about 70 years and was then relegated, like most samurai weapons, to ceremonial use. The weapon was still manufactured, but its technology quickly became obsolete when Japan reopened its doors to foreigners in the nineteenth century. The arquebus would look utterly medieval when compared with the modern guns aboard Commodore Perry's 'Black Ships' in 1852.

Right: Modern samurai armour was known as tōsei gusoku, and replaced the earlier, boxier yoroi. Tōsei gusoku armour was tailored and offered greater flexibility.

Ironically, the very last charge of the samurai, led by Saigo Takamori in 1877, would be on horseback with swords raised high against a line of firearm-carrying army regulars. And like the Takeda cavalry charge at the 1575 Battle of Nagashino, Takamori and his men would be decimated by gunfire. But it was not from a volley of arquebus musket balls delivered by a rotating front line, but instead by the rapid fire of a modern Gatling gun.

ARMOUR

'Every morning the samurai of 50 or 60 years ago would bathe, shave their foreheads, put lotion in their hair, cut their fingernails and toenails, rubbing them with pumice and then with wood sorrel, and without fail pay attention to their personal appearance. It goes without saying that their armour in general was kept free from rust, that it was dusted, shined and arranged.'

Miyamoto Musashi, *Go Rin No Sho*

The story of samurai armour is one of evolution from the early, lamellar suits – made up of layers of plates – worn by warriors on horseback, to the strong Sengoku Jidai cuirasses constructed to withstand arquebus shot. Traditional samurai armour was known as yoroi, or 'great armour'. Designed to be worn by a mounted samurai, yoroi

Left: This armour, which would have belonged to a high-ranking samurai, features a hoate face mask. The masks were designed to strike fear into the enemy.

typically had a box shape, weighed around 30kg (66lb) and hung down from the shoulders. Yoroi armour took the Asiatic lamellar style and was made from small iron or leather scales tied together and then lacquered to form plates. These horizontal plates were then tied in an overlapping fashion and attached at the back with laces.

Foot soldiers were given a simpler form of protection in the dō maru, a type of armoured jacket that was held in place by a belt. A similar armour that also laced at the back was called the haramaki. The haramaki and dō maru were lesser forms of armour, but offered significantly more flexibility than the yoroi. The yoroi was designed primarily for an archer, and was too rigid for swordplay. As a result, aspects of the three types of armour were brought together to create the tōsei gusoku, or modern armour. The most noticeable difference between the tōsei gusoku and the yoroi was the tailoring. The tōsei gusoku often tapered in at the waist and was designed for the hips to share the armour's weight, rather than the shoulders alone.

The most popular kind of tōsei gusoku was the okegawa dō, a strong, simple suit of armour designed to withstand the demands of the Sengoku Jidai. For the okegawa dō, the horizontal plates made up of thousands of smaller scales had been replaced by single plates made of one piece of

Wearing Samurai Armour

The process of donning samurai armour was described by Kayakawa Kyūkei in a 1735 manual called *Tanki Yoriaku: Hi Ko Ben*, which roughly translates as 'the art of armour wearing'. The descriptions for the various pieces of the pictured okegawa dō suit are based on Kyūkei's work and the 1911 notes of translator Matt Garbutt.

1. KABUTO (helmet)

There are hundreds of different styles of helmets and several different styles of shikoro, the neck guard hanging from the back and sides of the helmet. There are three varieties of cord to secure the helmet to the head.

2. HOATE (mask)

There are about six styles all to cover the cheek and chin. A movable nosepiece is recommended. Whiskers on the mask are not necessary, but it is desirable to have moustaches. Before putting on the mask place a handkerchief between the mask and the chin, then fasten the ends of the cords on top of your head.

3. SODE (shoulder plates)

Fasten them to the dō by means of hooks, and fasten first the left one and then the right, in each case the back one before the front. Large and medium sode are only worn by important officers.

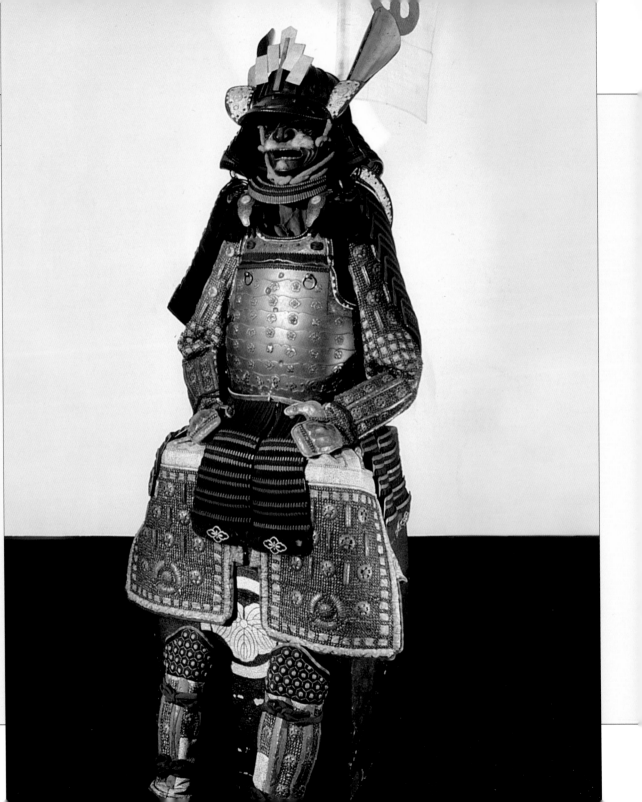

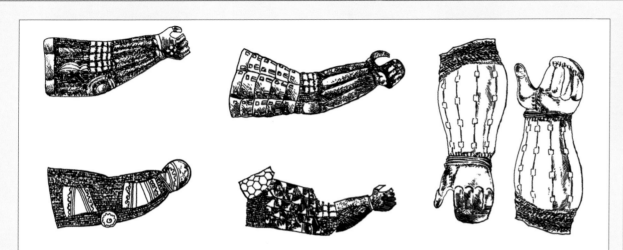

9. SUNEATE (shinguards)

A popular type in the Sengoku Period consists of vertical plates connected by either hinges or chainmail and often lined with textile material. There is always a leather guard that is affixed to the inner side at the place that comes in contact with the stirrup when riding. As usual, the left will be put on first.

4. DŌ (body armour) and KUSAZURI (skirts)

There are many kinds of dō. As will be seen, this piece comprises not only the back and breastplate but also the laminated skirt piece called kusazuri. The okegawa-dō is put on in six stages, from a sitting position.

5. KOTE (sleeves)

These sleeves are usually made of textile material, often silk brocade, padded, laced with small cords upon the inside of the arm and covered with mail, small metal plates or quilting. Do not pull the laces of the kote too tightly or the movement of the arm will be hampered. When shooting, take off your right kote.

6. YUGAKE (gloves)

Yugake are made of tanned skin and unlined ones are recommended. In donning these, the right should be put on first. The departure from the ordinary rule is because of the superior ability of the right hand and the difficulty of tying the cords after covering the left.

7. UWA-OBI (belt, sash)

For this, linen and cotton cloths are recommended wound twice or three times around the body, the actual length depending upon the wearer. Fold the linen or cotton cloth into halves, then twist it and put a little piece of leather in the centre, so that you can find the middle even when in a dark place.

8. HAIDATE (thighguards)

Haidate usually consist of an apron-like piece of cloth, having its lower part covered with small overlapping plates of metal or leather. A good way to wear the haidate is to tie the cords outside it. You can then move freely and still take it off quickly.

ROBES

Simple hitatare robes were worn under trousers and attached with laces at the knee. Straw sandals were often favoured because they were easy to replace and, unlike fur boots, did not house fleas and lice. Suneate shinguards were then tied on.

ARMOUR

A kusazuri skirt piece was attached to protect the legs, and then kote sleeves and yugake gloves were added. Padding for the arms was followed by the armour, which was secured in place with laces.

WEAPONS

Sode shoulder guards were attached, along with the swords, and a nodowa to protect the throat. A hachimaki head cloth was tied on, followed by the hoate face mask and finally the helmet.

Right: Haramaki armour was an armoured jacket that laced up at the back. The haramaki was a lesser form of armour worn by ashigaru footsoldiers.

leather or iron. The intricate system of back lacing had also been reduced. Eventually the laces would be replaced by steel rivets holding the plates together, either vertically or horizontally.

Armour lacing had caused huge problems for warring samurai who often had to wear their armour for weeks at a time. When wet, the lacing made the armour much heavier and it would often freeze in winter. The lacing was also difficult to wash free of the mud and filth collected on long campaigns. Suits would become infested with ants and lice and bring ill-health to the wearer. The metres of lacing present in the armour also caused enemy spears and arrows to catch on the armour instead of glancing off. Many samurai were therefore pleased to see laces largely replaced by rivets.

Protection from Arquebus Shot

The okegawa dō was practical, easy to wear and cheap to make. Because it was built with arquebuses in mind, many okegawa dō suits went out onto the battlefield already displaying dents where they had been tested against arquebus balls. As the armour contained fewer pieces than in its predecessors, okegawa dō could be produced quickly at a much lower cost. Okegawa dō were created in great numbers for the ashigaru. The front was often lacquered with the daimyō's colours and mon. Ashigaru not wearing an okegawa dō instead favoured a type of folding armour called tatami dō. This lightweight armour consisted of small connecting pieces of square metal that were often

sewn into a thick back lining. Worn as a kind of armoured apron, the tatami dō was tough and easy to collapse and carry when not in use.

Samurai retainers higher up the ranks favoured more elaborate okegawa dō suits. To make sure they were noticed on the battlefield, warriors often embellished their armour with striking colours, eye-catching patterns, emblems and even pictures. Other more bizarre suits were constructed to look like naked torsos, complete with rows of ribs and rounded Buddha bellies.

Helmets and masks

'Furthermore, while ornamentation on armour is unnecessary, one should be very careful about the appearance of his helmet. It is something that accompanies his head to the enemy's camp.'

Miyamoto Musashi, *Go Rin No Sho*

Although sword master Miyamoto Musashi advised against the ornamentation of samurai armour, it was a trend that became more ostentatious as time went on. And while warriors liked to customize their armour so that they were seen on the battlefield, the use of elaborate headgear really allowed them to stand out from the mass.

The samurai helmet, or kabuto, consisted of a bowl constructed from up to 32 curved plates that were riveted together. The simplest helmets, made up of eight plates, were called helmets 'for a hundred heads'. As the name suggests, these were mass-produced and worn mostly by the ashigaru. At the other end of the scale were the helmets of different

Facing page: From the mid-sixteenth century, crests on helmets were commonplace. Here, a replica of Toyotomi Hideyoshi's helmet is shown with its distinct 'sunburst' crest.

Left: A kawari kabuto decorative helmet featuring a mythical sea creature on top. Helmet ornaments were often constructed from lacquered papier-mâché.

shapes, helmets with elaborate crests and helmets with whole sculptures built on top.

Before the Sengoku Jidai, only high-ranking samurai would attach a crest to the visor of their helmet, but from the mid-sixteenth century crests were commonplace. Made from papier-mâché, crests would take various shapes, including antlers, wild boars, peacock feathers, crescent moons, butterflies and stylized centipedes. The most famous of these was a rear 'sunburst' crest worn by Toyomoti Hideyoshi, making him an unmistakable figure on the field of battle.

The mid-sixteenth century also saw the rise of kawari kabuto, a decorative helmet only available to high-ranking samurai who could afford it. The kawari kabuto took different shapes, such as 'peach' and 'acorn', and were often adorned with large ornamental sculptures. These were made from iron and wooden frames with lacquered papier-mâché and covered in an extraordinary individualistic array, from fins to sea monsters, rabbit ears, crabs and cow horns. The cow horns were worn by none other than Tokugawa Ieyasu, who had the horns fitted along with cow hair after he heard that Toyotomi referred to him as the 'Cow of the Kanto'. The famous samurai general of the Korean invasion, Katō Kiyomasa, sported a silver kawari kabuto with a tall, elongated fin and a red sun disc on either side.

Wearing a Helmet

There are hundreds of different styles of helmets and several different styles of shikoro, the neck guard hanging from the back and sides of the helmet. To put on the helmet:

1. Hold the cords under the ears of the helmet, placing your thumbs inside the helmet and all your fingers outside. Lift the helmet above your head, put it on from behind and pull it forwards.

2. Pull the front loop of the helmet cord and put it under your chin.

3. Put both ends of the main cord through the metal rings inside the helmet to catch the cords and pull them upwards.

4. Pull them towards your ears and pass them through the other cords, which are arranged inside the helmet.

5. Pull the cords downwards and tie them under your chin.

6. Twist the ends of the cords that are already tied and then tuck them between the cheeks of the mask.

From *Tanki Yoriaku: Hi Ko Ben*, by Hayakawa Kyūkei (1735), translated by Matt Garbutt 1911.

Ceremonial Armour

The purpose of the kawari kabuto was to show a samurai's rank, social standing and wealth. They were also intended to intimidate the enemy, although the sculptures themselves were entirely useless in adding protection. During the Edo Period of peace, kawari kabutos, and indeed all samurai armour, became less functional and more ceremonial. Both kabuto and armour became even more elaborate at this time, with their main purpose being to impress others. Many suits of armour from this period even returned to the earlier laced models that had proved so hazardous on the battlefield.

Facemasks

Facemasks were commonly known as hoate, and were attached to the kabuto. These masks were designed primarily to intimidate an opponent, and often featured a fierce expression and a sinister, grinning mouth. The inside of the mask was sometimes lacquered in red to give the wearer's face a more striking hue. A moustache made of horsehair was often applied under the nose. Beneath this, on the underside of the chin, a hole was drilled to allow sweat to drain out. Some of the masks covered the whole face and others just the nose, chin and cheeks. Masks for the whole face commonly had a detachable nose, which indicates

Left: There were around six styles of hoate face masks. Throat protection was often attached to the bottom of the mask, as shown.

Facing page: High-ranking samurai sometimes opted to adorn their helmets with cow horns, rabbit ears and centipedes. Honda Tadatomo famously wore deer antlers on his helmet.

Left: This hoate face mask features a horsehair moustache and a removable nose piece. A small hole underneath the chin enabled sweat to drain out.

the difficulty with breathing. In most respects masks were actually considered a hindrance to combat: they made it harder to see or breathe properly and provided little protection. On the plus side, a mask acted as a buffer between the cords on the helmet and the underside of the wearer's chin, an area often afflicted by chafing. A mask would also allow for a plated bib called a yodarekake to be hung from the bottom. This would provide excellent protection for the throat and could be used instead of the normal nodowa, usually a type of metal ring that was attached around the throat.

The nodowa was a useful piece of equipment, as this story describes:

'In 1564 on the seventh day of the first month, two battles took place at Kōnodai, in Shimōsa, between Hōjō Ujiyasu and Satomi Yoshihiro, assisted by Ota Sukemasa, Niudo Sanrakusai, in which the Hōjō forces were victorious. Ota fought desperately and had received two wounds, when Shimizu Tarozayemon, a man noted for his strength, threw down the now weary Oda, but tried in vain to cut off his head.

At this, Ota cried out, "Are you flurried, sir? My neck is protected by a nodowa. Remove it, and take off my head." Shimizu replied with a bow: "How kind you are to tell me! You die a noble death. You have my admiration!" But, just as he was about to remove the nodowa, two young squires of Ota rushed up, and throwing Shimizu down, enabled their master to decapitate him.'

Tanki Yoriaku: Hi Ko Ben by Kayakawa Kyūkei 1735, translated by Matt Garbutt 1911

Miscellaneous Samurai Equipment

In addition to a samurai's armour and weaponry the Tanki Yoriaku: Hi Ko Ben recommends carrying the following equipment:

Sashimono (little flag)

There are hundreds of different kinds of sashimono, generally made of silk. Sashimono are usually vertical oblongs 91cm by 30cm (3ft by 1ft). The back of the dō carried at the waistline is a socket and at the level of the shoulder blades a small hinged bridge-piece, having on it a ring. These were to support the sashimono.

Kate-Bukuro (provision bag)

For ordinary officers the koshi-dzuto is recommended; it is made of twisted paper strings and measures about 1ft by 9.5in [30cm by 24cm]. It is carried at the right side of the waist. Besides this it is advisable to carry another bag in which are three to four gou of rice. In cold weather baked rice is recommended because it gives warmth.

Gunsen (folding war fan)

A light one is recommended. You can carry it at your waist or hang it to the ring on the upper part of the breastplate, but when in actual fighting do not hang it on the chest as it is then very inconvenient in using the sword or bow and arrow. These fans have the outer sticks usually of iron, the inner ones of yellow metal.

Koshinawa (rope)

About 5ft [1.5m] long, the kind called kara-uchi-no-himo is the best for the purpose. Fasten a ring or loop to one of the ends, and carry it either fastened to the sword scabbard or on the right side of the waist. This cord is useful in many ways, as, for instance, securing a saddle, tethering a horse or binding a prisoner.

Kubibukuro (head bag)

A bag made of netting to carry the severed head of an enemy. When walking carry it hung to your waist, when mounted fasten it to the saddle.

Naga tenugui (long towel)

Of white cotton about 5ft [1.5m] long, carried attached to the sword-scabbard. It is used for such purposes as bandaging wounds, carrying provisions, wrapping up a bow or musket, or as a turban, a tasuki for girdling up the sleeves or in an emergency as a substitute sashimono.

From *Tanki Yoriaku: Hi Ko Ben* by Kayakawa Kyūkei 1735, translated by Matt Garbutt 1911

Below: A sashimono was a flag depicting a samurai's family name or clan emblem. Attaching the sashimono to the warrior's armour freed his hands up for fighting.

Above: A folding war fan made from iron, metal or wood was used for signalling and fighting. It hung from the samurai's breastplate when he was marching.

Myth and Reality of the Samurai

The popular view of the samurai warrior is of an unswervingly loyal, stoic, self-sacrificing swordsman who is honest, honourable and heroic on the battlefield. When not at war, this warrior is a cultivated and refined gentleman, as accomplished in calligraphy, falconry and tea ceremonies as he is in removing the heads of his enemies. This model of the samurai is a staple of popular culture, appearing often in comic books, video games, television and movies. Hollywood films in particular celebrate the philosophical aspects of the samurai ethos, often meeting heavy criticism in Japan.

One Japanese reviewer noted that the samurai character of Katsumoto in the 2003 film *The Last Samurai* was so pious that he 'set my teeth on edge.' Similarly, a 2013 film that aimed to recast the story of the 47 rōnin bombed in Japan. This legend and its

Facing page: In Akira Kurosawa's *Seven Samurai*, the character Kambei sums up the meaningless existence of the rōnin: 'Again we are defeated. The farmers have won, not us.'

Right: Despite being a samurai pretender, the *Seven Samurai* character Kikuchiyo displays many of the virtues inherent in Bushidō, including loyalty, honour and fearlessness in battle.

ideals of loyalty and self-sacrifice are of such pivotal importance to Japanese culture that the retelling of the story even has its own term: Chūshingura. But it is not just Western movies that perpetuate myths about the samurai ideal. One of the heroes of Akira Kurosawa's 1954 film *Seven Samurai* – widely considered one of the great samurai movies of all time – is Kyūzō, a stoic master swordsman who rejects praise for his heroic deeds along with his tot of pre-battle sake.

The tradition of celebrating the honourable and civilized aspects of the samurai, however, is far older than Kurosawa. The samurai themselves first began codifying their ideals and ethos as bushidō,

Bushidō and Belief

Foreign interest in the bushidō ethos was first sparked by Nitobe Inazō's *Bushidō, The Soul of Japan* published in 1900. The book, written in English, was a great favourite among overseas readers and compared aspects of samurai bushidō to medieval chivalry and Homer's *Iliad*. The four religious tenets of bushidō are described by Inazō below.

BUDDHISM
'It furnished a sense of calm trust in Fate, a quiet submission to the inevitable, that stoic composure in sight of danger, or calamity, that disdain of life and friendliness with death.'

ZEN
'Its method is contemplation, and its purport, to be convinced of a principle that underlies all phenomena, and, if it can, of the Absolute itself, and thus to put oneself in harmony with this Absolute… whoever attains to the perception of the Absolute raises himself above mundane things.'

SHINTŌ
'The tenets of Shintōism cover the two predominating features of the emotional life of our race – Patriotism and Loyalty… Such loyalty to the sovereign, such reverence for ancestral memory, and such filial piety as are not taught by any other creed, were inculcated by the Shintō doctrines, imparting passivity to the otherwise arrogant nature of the samurai.'

Above: Nitobe Inazō's *Bushidō: The Soul of Japan* explained samurai culture and ethos for Western readers.

CONFUCIANISM
'The teachings of Confucius were the most prolific source of Bushidō. His enunciation of the five moral relations between master and servant (the governing and the governed), father and son, husband and wife, older and younger brother, and between friend and friend, was but a confirmation of what the race instinct had recognized before his writings were introduced from China.'

Bushidō, The Soul of Japan, Nitobe Inazō, 1900

or 'Way of the Warrior'. Bushidō was the code of ethics that every samurai was expected to live and die by. It required a spirit of courage and fearlessness alongside the virtues of loyalty, honour, rectitude, integrity, benevolence, obedience, honesty, duty, filial piety (duty to one's family) and self-sacrifice. These bushidō ideals were heavily influenced by the belief systems of Buddhism, Zen, Confucianism and Shintō. Buddhism taught a warrior not to fear death, as he would be reincarnated in the next life. Zen helped a warrior to 'empty his mind' and maintain clarity in battle. Confucianism encouraged morality, self-sacrifice and filial piety. Shintō idealized loyalty, patriotism and ancestor-worship.

Above: Minamoto Yoshitsune faces down the approaching Taira fleet. Despite his heroic image, Yoshitsune was not skilled with a bow and ended up dropping it in the sea.

Right: Tea ceremonies were a great favourite with Toyotomi Hideyoshi, although he ordered his tea ceremony master Sen no Rikyū to commit seppuku.

Bushidō Beginnings

The foundation for the bushidō ideology was laid in the ninth century, when a warrior's most valued attributes were his military skills and fortitude in war. But it was not long before the samurai were expected to be more than just courageous fighters. The best warriors were eulogized in the early medieval war chronicle the *Heike Monogatari* as self-sacrificing, respectful and utterly devoted to their clan. By the fourteenth century, chivalric virtues began to appear in Japanese texts. From then on samurai were encouraged to combine their military prowess with kindness, frugality, honesty and integrity. These principles became an integral part of the samurai code, which from the seventeenth century had a name – bushidō.

It was therefore during the seventeenth century, and the ensuing 250 years of peace ushered in by Tokugawa Ieyasu, that texts on bushidō began to appear in great quantities. At this time, when warriors were left without wars to fight, there was a great need to define the samurai's purpose in the modern world. Ieyasu himself encouraged samurai forays into the cultural pursuits of poetry, calligraphy and tea ceremonies to distract the warriors and give balance to their more bloodthirsty attributes. Ieyasu also promulgated the study of Confucianism as a way of civilizing samurai warriors and preparing them for their new role as administrators of peacetime Japan.

Hagakure

While many of the seventeenth-century bushidō texts were theory-led, the most popular book of the day claimed that the Way of the Warrior could be found only in death. *Hagakure*, or 'Fallen Leaves', was samurai Yamamoto Tsunetomo's version of the Way of the Warrior, published some years after his death in 1719. *Hagakure* was a favourite among Edo Period warriors as it contradicted contemporary bushidō texts that focused on chivalry and gentlemanly values. Instead, *Hagakure* argued that a warrior's life should be devoted to one's master and the preparation for death. The text begins:

'Although it stands to reason that a samurai should be mindful of the Way of the Samurai, it would seem we are all negligent. Consequently, if someone were to ask, "What is the true meaning of the Way of the Samurai?" the person who would be able to answer promptly is rare. This is because it has not been established in one's mind beforehand. From this, unmindfulness of the Way can be known… The Way of the Samurai is found in death. When it comes to either/or, there is only the choice of death. It is not particularly difficult. Be determined and advance. To say that dying without reaching one's aim is to die a dog's death is the frivolous way of sophisticates. When pressed with the choice of life or death, it is not necessary to gain one's aim.'

Hagakure: The Way of the Samurai, Yamamoto Tsunetomo

Above: *Hagakure* **was a great favourite among samurai warriors: it proclaimed the 'Way of the Warrior' could be found only in death.**

Bushidō literature from the seventeenth century is therefore often highly philosophical. There is also a variety of texts from this time, with different writers expressing the ethos, background and application of bushidō in different proportions. Usually, special emphasis was placed on the samurai conducting themselves as refined and cultivated warriors, with long sections on the new application of their martial principles in peacetime. In other words, the texts often concentrated on *what* it meant to be a samurai warrior, rather than providing practical military applications of *how to perform as one*.

Part of the burgeoning theory of bushidō during the Edo Period was to consider the samurai heroes of the past, and romanticize their 'great deeds' in an attempt to make warriors of the day behave properly. The heroic exploits of past great samurai were recounted with sentimental flourishes in artworks, poems, plays and books. These warriors usually appeared to be bushidō purists: cultivated, unshakably loyal, self-sacrificing, educated in the arts of war, indomitable on the battlefield and, oddly, often fated to lose.

Loyalty as Virtue

An often-cited example is Kusunoki Masashige, a legendary fourteenth-century Japanese warrior and a great exemplar of loyalty and self-sacrifice. Masashige became a legend when he was ordered by Emperor Go-Daigo to lead an army into a battle he knew could not be won. But, rather than refuse his master or even question his logic, Masashige marched off to his death. After his assessment was

proved correct and the battle lost, Masashige, his brother and a handful of samurai retainers took refuge in an abandoned farmhouse as the enemy closed in. It was here they all committed seppuku, but before making the final cut, Masashige and his brother lamented not having seven more lives to devote to the Emperor's service.

Fidelity until death was considered the most important bushidō virtue, but there was also a particular appeal in the blindly loyal samurai who had been betrayed and outcast. One example was Minamoto Yoshitsune, the samurai hero of the twelfth century Gempei War and the subject of countless books, plays and poems. Like Masashige, Yoshitsune was something of a samurai archetype: refined, educated and trained in the arts of war; young, dashing and successful with women; loyal and self-sacrificing. But in the end he was doomed to failure. It is this last point that appears to make Yoshitsune such an attractive historical figure in Japan. Despite winning the Gempei War on behalf of the Minamoto and being blindly devoted to his clan leader and brother Yoritomo, Yoshitsune's destiny is to be condemned as an outlaw.

Myth and Legend

The fatal appeal of the lone, ostracized samurai is a celebrated theme in Japanese folklore. Yoshitsune's story is also an example of when the line between

Left: Minamoto Yoshiie was considered the eleventh century's quintessential samurai warrior: he was cultured, fearless and usually respectful of his enemies.

Facing page: Warrior-monk Benkei swore his lifelong allegiance to Minamoto Yoshitsune, after Yoshitsune defeated him in hand-to-hand combat on the Gojo Bridge in Kyoto.

fact and fiction in samurai legend become blurred, as the tale crosses over into mythology. A good example is Yoshitsune's right-hand man Benkei, a 1.9m- (6ft 6in-) giant with wild hair and godlike strength who never leaves Yoshitsune's side. It is Benkei who holds off an army of attackers in the couple's final hour so that Yoshitsune is able to commit seppuku. Although his body is riddled with arrows, Benkei remains standing until a horseman knocks him down – he has been dead for some time but continues to stand guard for his master, even in death.

As Benkei was mythologized through the ages, he became something of an impossible figure in his virtuousness. Most samurai could maintain some of the tenets of bushidō while letting others slip. One such case is Minamoto Yoshiie, considered the eleventh century's quintessential samurai warrior. Yoshiie was a formidable soldier and a cultured and respected leader who famously chased down his fleeing opponent Abe Sadato after the fall of his Koromo Castle. Sadato was wounded and tried to escape his pursuer, but Yoshiie asked, 'Wasn't he ashamed to turn his back on his enemy who had a message for him?' Sadato then turned to face Yoshiie, who did not draw his sword but instead recited a verse from a poem: 'The warps of your robe have come undone,' which meant Sadato's castle had been destroyed. To this Sadato called back a subsequent verse from the same poem: 'Over the years its threads became tangled, and this pains me.' And with this gentlemanly exchange, Yoshiie let his enemy go, deeming this the honourable thing

Katō's Way

While many writers of bushidō theorized about its philosophical heart, other samurai theorists found no problem deciding how warriors should conduct themselves. Daimyō Katō Kiyomasa laid out his version of the 'Way' for his samurai in a simple set of rules and regulations called the 'Precepts of Katō Kiyomasa':

Codes that all samurai should follow, regardless of rank:

• One should not be negligent in the way of the retainer. One should rise at four in the morning, practise sword technique, eat one's meal and train with the bow, the gun and the horse. A well-developed retainer should become even more so.

• If one should want diversions, he should make them outdoor pastimes such as falcony, deer hunting and wrestling.

• For clothing, anything between cotton and natural silk will do. A man who squanders money for clothing and brings his household finances into disorder is fit for punishment. Generally one should concern oneself with armour appropriate for his social position and use his money for martial affairs.

• When associating with one's ordinary companions, one should limit the meeting to one guest and one host, and the meal should consist of plain brown rice.

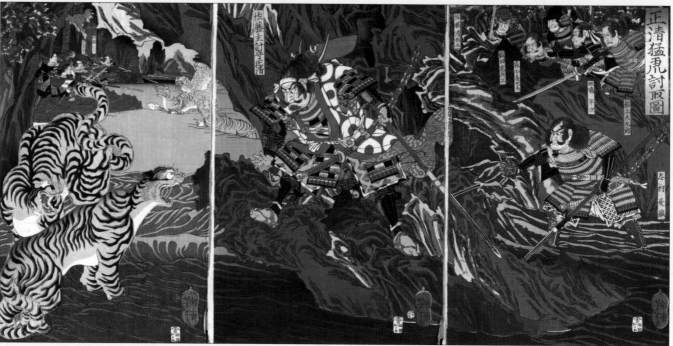

Above: Katō Kiyomasa famously hunted tigers while invading the northern territories of Korea.

When practising the martial arts, however, one may meet with many people.

• As for decorum at the time of a campaign, one must be mindful that he is a samurai. A person who loves beautification where it is unnecessary is fit for punishment.

• The practice of Noh Drama is absolutely forbidden.

When one unsheathes his sword, he has cutting a person down on his mind. Thus, as all things are born from being placed in one's heart, a samurai who practises dancing, which is outside of the martial arts, should be ordered to commit seppuku.

• One should put forth great effort in matters of learning. One should read books concerning military matters, and direct his attention exclusively to the virtues of loyalty and filial piety. Reading Chinese poetry, linked verse and waka is forbidden. One will surely become womanized

Above: Katō Kiyomasa set out strict rules of behaviour for his samurai: any found dancing would be ordered to commit seppuku.

if he gives his heart knowledge of such elegant and delicate refinements. Having been born into the house of a warrior, one's intentions should be to grasp the long and the short swords and to die.

- If a man does not investigate the matter of bushidō daily, it will be difficult for him to die a brave and manly death. Thus it is essential to engrave this business of the warrior into one's mind well.

- The above conditions should be adhered to night and day. If there is anyone who finds these conditions difficult to fulfill, he should be dismissed, an investigation should be quickly carried out, it should be signed and sealed that he was unable to mature in the Way of Manhood, and he should be driven out. On this, there can be no doubt.

to do. But Yoshiie then belies his bushidō virtues by becoming the first samurai warlord to openly challenge the Emperor. The incident occurs when the Emperor tells Yoshiie he is not allowed to kill his prisoners of war. Enraged at this order, Yoshiie decapitates his prisoners and throws their heads into a ditch by the side of the road. Considered a grave insult to the victims of the families as well as a display of defiance towards the Emperor, it is

Above: The Mongol invasion showed the samurai that their traditional notions of honour in warfare were of little interest to foreign invaders.

146

Below: Arquebuses were notoriously clumsy to fire and reload. Well-organized armies employed assistants to help with gunpowder and ammunition.

Facing page: Samurai warriors were expected to die an honourable death by the sword. Those defeated in battle could retain their honour by committing seppuku.

difficult to see where the 'gentlemanly' Yoshiie's bushidō ethics lie in these actions.

In this way, the whole notion of bushidō, even among those legendary warriors who valiantly beheld its virtues, is riddled with contradictions. Simply, there were no guarantees that those cultivated samurai, well-versed in etiquette and tradition, would actually behave honourably.

Honour was one of the key virtues of the bushidō code, but it often gave way to ambition and self-interest. The codes of bushidō were also sometimes inconsistent in their messages about honour. Those considered the best warriors, for example, were the ones who had put the conditions of warfare to their advantage. Samurai were encouraged to be opportunists in war – such as fighting with the sun at their back so it would blind their opponent – but they were also paradoxically expected to conduct a fair fight.

Loyalty was another elusive ideal, although in theory it was the pre-eminent quality of the samurai, prized above all else. Any worthy warrior would follow his master into death or lay down his life for him. But loyalty to *whom*, or *what*, was another question. The Emperor was considered to be the most important man in Japan, until the provincial clans decided they did not want to serve him. He was then replaced with a Shōgun, or regent. But Shōguns, too, were capable of disloyalty. Samurai would

follow their Shōgun or clan leader to the ends of the earth, but their fidelity was often rewarded with death or betrayal. Loyalty to one's clan was thought an essential, but brothers would not hesitate to kill each other to better their position.

The stories of the greatest samurai heroes are therefore parables of loyalty to one's clan, one's Emperor, one's master and oneself, which don't reflect the darker reality. It is the complex relationship with this topmost bushidō virtue that defined the legacies of these samurai, but their actions often confuse rather than clarify the ethos of bushidō.

Searching for Sengoku Bushidō

While epic texts extolled the bushidō exploits of ancient samurai, similar versions about the warriors of the 1467–1615 Sengoku Jidai are less easy to find. This is in part because the ideals of warfare changed following the failed Mongol invasions of Japan in the thirteenth century. This was the first time the samurai had to contend with a foreign enemy, and they soon found that their opponents cared little for battleground etiquette or honour in warfare. The Mongols committed terrible atrocities against the civilians of Tsushima Island, who they then hanged on the masts of their ships. When the samurai on Kyūshū saw their half-dead compatriots suspended from the Mongol ships sailing towards them, notions

Right: Takeda Shingen was among the last of the old guard of samurai gentlemen. He is seen here (top centre) in a war council with his generals.

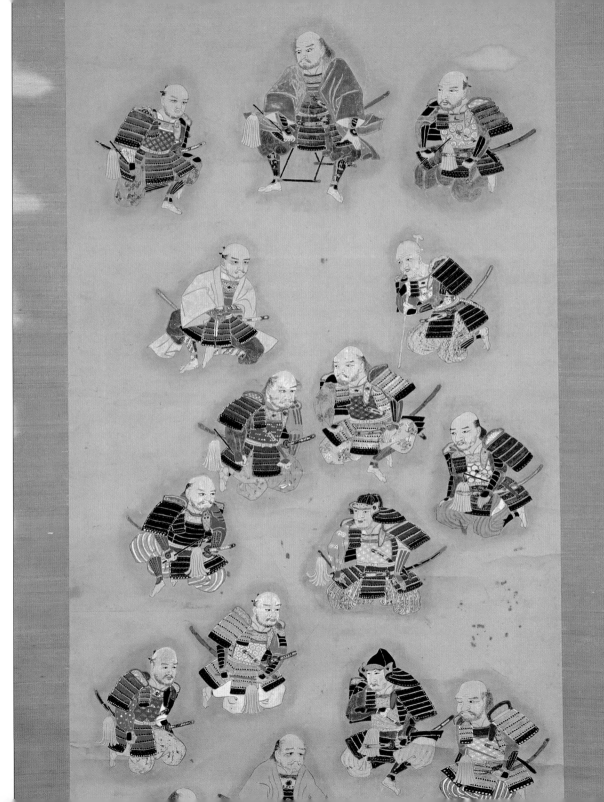

of whistling arrows to begin mounted duels quickly became irrelevant. A further shock was the advanced Mongol weaponry – volleys of poisoned arrows and exploding iron bombs hurled by large catapults.

The use of gunpowder in battle became a common feature of samurai warfare when it was introduced to Japan in the mid-sixteenth century. In effect this made the methods of warfare of old defunct. The purpose behind a mounted duel was for two gentleman warriors of equal rank and social standing to meet for consensual combat. This was considered the honourable way to allow for a samurai of standing to die, but now one could be killed by a lowly foot soldier. This amounted to a considerable loss of face for the deceased warrior's family – and the introduction of the arquebus ensured it happened on a regular basis.

Upholding Tradition

Despite the establishment of the arquebus on the field of combat, two opposing generals maintained battle decorum according to the traditions of old. Takeda Shingen and Uesugi Kenshin made sure their army met at the same place to do battle every year, and would withdraw their forces out of respect if one side appeared to have the upper hand. Uesugi Kenshin also supplied Takeda Shingen with salt during a campaign when he heard his counterpart had run out. Kenshin was said to have sat and wept when news reached him of Shingen's demise.

In the end the Takeda were outdone by Oda Nobunaga's forces, which used brand new arquebuses to deadly effect. Gentlemanly generals like Shingen and Kenshin quickly became outdated when pitted against the upstarts Nobunaga, Toyotomi Hideyoshi and Tokugawa Ieyasu. It was during their reigns that the role of the samurai changed, as the 'low overcame the high' and noble pretensions became secondary to victory and the seizure of power. The final outcome of this was the rise of bushidō in the public consciousness and its codification during the Tokugawa Shōgunate. But what about the role of bushidō during the time of Nobunaga, Hideyoshi and Ieyasu? Did the essential tenets of bushidō – honour, bravery, integrity, loyalty, self-sacrifice, filial piety – make an appearance during this time, or were they only associated with their predecessors, the samurai warriors of old?

Below: A statue of Takeda Shingen, who in the end was entirely undone by the gekokujō upstarts Oda Nobunaga and Tokugawa Ieyasu.

**Above: Torii Suneemon heroically crept past the Takedas'
traps to raise the alarm for Nagashino Castle. But the
Takeda ensnared him on his return.**

Bravery was certainly never lacking during
the history of the samurai, and often it was found
coupled with self-sacrifice. A good example occurs
during the build-up to the 1575 Battle of Nagashino.
Here, surrounded by besieging Takeda retainers,

Torii Suneemon managed to creep past the enemy
and run through the night to alert Nobunaga. But
Suneemon was caught as he tried to re-enter the
castle and was made an offer for his life. So, tied to a
cross and lifted up to the walls of Nagashino Castle

Right: Oda Nobunaga is pictured here at the Battle of Okehazama. Nobunaga's historic victory at Okehazama heralded the start of his meteoric rise to the top.

with a spear at his ribs, Suneemon had the chance to lie to the inhabitants and tell them that no help was on its way, and live; or, tell them Nobunaga was coming and lose his life. Like a true samurai, Suneemon chose death.

Integrity and honour were harder to find in the sixteenth century, and there are certainly many examples of their absence. Oda Nobunaga ordered the murder of thousands of innocent men, women and children in the monastery at Mount Hiei and the razing of Nagashima Castle. None of its 20,000 inhabitants escape the flames. Nobunaga's successor Toyotomi Hideyoshi was also guilty of heinous crimes against the code of bushidō. He commanded his tea ceremony master Sen no Rikyū to commit seppuku on a whim, and then forced his heir Hidetsugu to do the same. He then ordered the public execution of Hidetsugu's young children and 30 women who had served him. Hideyoshi's courage in war was legendary, but in his last days he often ordered the beating to death of any attendant who annoyed him.

Power Struggles

Tokugawa Ieyasu was little better. He famously broke his deathbed promise to his predecessor Hideyoshi by warring with his heir Hideyori so he could seize power for himself. He later trained his cannon on the residential quarters during

Above: A samurai committing seppuku, or 'belly-slitting'. Those warriors who left some of their viscera hanging from the wound were considered the bravest.

Death in Defeat

Seppuku could also be a collective act following defeat in battle. An early example of this came at the end of the 1333 Battle of Kamakura, when the Hōjō-occupied city was overrun by samurai loyal to Emperor Go-Daigo. Thousands of inhabitants killed themselves as a result, as recorded in the medieval epic the *Taiheiki*:

'Now Nagasaki Takashige ran around to this place saying, "kill yourselves quickly! I shall go before you as your example!" He stripped off the stomach armor which alone remained on his body, caused his younger brother to serve him wine in a cup that had been placed before the Lord of Sagami, drank three times and put down the cup in front of the lay monk Dojun of Settsu, saying, "To you do I give the cup, with this relish!" And he cut his body with a long cut from left to right and fell down, pulling out his inwards in front of Dojun. Dojun took up the cup, jesting, "Ah, what a relish! However abstemious a man might be, he would not refuse to drink this!" He drank half of the wine therein, put down the cup in front of the Suwa lay monk and in the same way cut his belly and died. When with tranquil spirit the lay monk Suwa Jikisho had tipped the cup three times, he put it down in front of His Lordship the Sagami lay monk, saying: "Most fully have the young men displayed their loyalty. It will not do for others to be idle, or to say, 'I am ripe in years.' From this time forth, let all eat of this repast!" He cut open his belly in a cross, drew forth the dagger again and laid it down before His Lordship the lay monk. Now the lay monk Nagasaki Enki had delayed to cut his belly, by reason that he looked with anxious eyes upon the Sagami lay monk. But Nagasaki Shin'uemon, a young boy 15 years old that year, bowed before his grandfather, saying: "Assuredly will the Buddhas and gods give sanction to this deed. The filial descendant is he who brings honour to the name of his fathers." With two thrusts of his dagger he slashed the veins of his aged grandfather's arms. He cut his own belly, pushed his grandfather down and fell on top of him. Thereupon the Sagami lay monk also cut his belly, urged to duty by this youth newly come of age, and the castle lay monk did the same, while in the hall Hōjō kinsmen and men of other houses bared their snowy skins to the waist, some cutting open their bellies and some striking off their own heads. Truly 283 of the Hōjō took their lives, each striving to be first.'

Taiheiki: A Chronicle of Medieval Japan, Translated by Helen Craig McCullough, 1959

Left: The Hōjō Takatoki Harakiri Yagura is one of the sites where the citizens of Kamakura performed mass suicide by seppuku.

the Siege of Ōsaka because he knew Hideyori's mother would be seeking refuge there. But Ieyasu, Hideyoshi and Nobunaga were not alone in their misdeeds. Disloyalty, in particular, was a common trait among the generals and daimyō of the age. One of Nobunaga's generals, Akechi Mitsuhide, committed the ultimate betrayal when he ordered his men to assassinate their commander in 1582. Nobunaga, as if to counterpoint Mitsuhide's crime, did the honourable thing according to bushidō and committed seppuku in the face of death.

If the sixteenth and the early seventeenth century present many examples of the tenets of bushidō being broken, the honourable death by seppuku still remains a reliable constant. The period often includes examples of seppuku by men otherwise bereft of bushidō virtue. Shibata Katsuie, who, for example, broke the terms of the Kiyosu conference and attacked his ally Hideyoshi, committed seppuku alongside his family and 80 retainers when he faced defeat. Katsuie's partner in crime, Oda Nobutaka, a man lacking not only in integrity, bravery and loyalty but also common sense, followed Katsuie's example of honour in death.

SEPPUKU

Seppuku, or suicide through belly-slitting, often known as hari-kiri, is the source of endless fascination in the West. The notion of honour in death by suicide was somehow legitimized in samurai culture by making the act itself as painful as possible. Seppuku involved plunging a blade

into the left abdomen, directly below the navel, and then dragging it across to the right side before making a final pull upwards. The bravest samurai were those who left their innards exposed or, better still, hanging from the wound. Because seppuku is such an agonizingly slow way to die, a second was often on hand to put the samurai out his misery by beheading him.

The earliest examples of seppuku were by samurai cornered by their enemy and faced with torture and crucifixion if caught. Later, seppuku was often used as a symbolic act to reduce shame, restore honour and avoid accusations of cowardice. Disgraced samurai would also commit seppuku to show their contrition, or as a form of protest – or simply because they were ordered to do so.

Seppuku was often a display of devotion to one's master. Here it was particularly revered as a display of the bushidō ideals of loyalty and self-sacrifice. This type of seppuku even had its own name: junshi, or 'death through fidelity'. Junshi was considered the most loyal act a samurai could perform. A famous case was that of Kusunoki Masashige. But another concerned Tomoe Gozen, one of the few women samurai recorded in Japanese history. According to the medieval epic the *Heike Monotagari*, Gozen 'had long black hair and a fair complexion, and her face was very lovely; moreover she was a fearless rider whom neither the fiercest horse nor the roughest ground could dismay, and so dexterously did she handle sword and bow that she was a match for a thousand warriors.'

But the *Heike Monogatari* has little to say about Gozen's life other than her exploits during the last stand of her master Minamoto Yoshinaka:

'But now they were reduced to but five survivors, and among these Tomoe still held her place. Calling her to him Kiso [Yoshinaka] said: "As you are a woman, it were better that you now make your escape. I have made up my mind to die, either by the hand of the enemy or by mine own, and how would Kiso be shamed if in his last fight he died with a woman?" Even at these strong words, however, Tomoe would not forsake him, but still feeling full of fight, she replied: "Ah, for some bold warrior to match with, that Kiso might see how fine a death I can die." And she drew aside her horse and waited. Presently Onda-no-Hachiro Moroshige of Musashi, a strong and valiant samurai, came riding up with 30 followers, and Tomoe, immediately dashing into them, flung herself upon Onda and grappling with him dragged him from his horse, pressed him calmly against the pommel of her saddle and cut off his head. Then stripping off her armour she fled away to the Eastern Provinces.'

The *Heike Monogatari*, translated by A. L. Sadler, 1918

Facing page: Tomoe Gozen was a famous female samurai. She is seen here battling an assailant during the last stand of her master, Minamoto Yoshinaka.

Below: A statue of Tomoe Gozen alongside Minamoto Yoshinaka. According to legend, Gozen committed suicide upon hearing of Yoshinaka's death.

156

Tomoe's last act of service to Yoshinaka was that of junshi. The accounts seldom agree on the exact nature of her suicide, but the most popular has Tomoe jumping into the sea and drowning herself after hearing of Yoshinaka's death. It is perhaps surprising that instances of junshi became more frequent during the Edo Period of peace than they did during times of war. One of the most celebrated examples of junshi occurred at the start of the eighteenth century, as part of the story of the 47 rōnin.

The 47 Rōnin

The story of the 47 rōnin began in 1701, when daimyō Asano Naganori was visiting Edo Castle. The Master of Ceremonies was Kira Yoshinaka, a man who needed to be properly bribed to ensure the visit went smoothly. But Naganori, a devout Confucian, did not believe in bribes and his subsequent gift to Yoshinaka was deemed insultingly cheap. Yoshinaka decided to challenge and humiliate him. He openly mocked the daimyō and made faces at him, until an enraged Naganori attacked Yoshinaka with his wakizashi. Luckily Naganori was pulled off Yoshinaka before he was seriously hurt, but the castle official did receive

a cut to the face. Although the injury was minor, Naganori had committed a grave offense by unsheathing his dagger in the Shōgun's castle, and he was ordered to commit seppuku. The Shōgun then ordered that there should be no retaliation.

Naganori's death, however, left 47 of his retainers without a master. These men were honour-bound to take revenge, but the tale of their vengeance involved an extended pause. Yoshinaka was expecting an immediate reprisal for his part in Naganori's death, and had put the rōnin under surveillance. The leader of the 47 rōnin, Ōishi Yoshio, knew they were being watched by Yoshinaka's spies and ordered the group to disband and move to separate parts of the country. For his part, Yoshio moved to Kyoto and began disgracing himself by drinking heavily, brawling and visiting geisha houses. He played the part of the fallen warrior so well that a passing Satsuma man kicked him and spat on him in disgust after he had passed out drunk in the gutter. Reports of Yoshio's debauchery reached Yoshinaka, and after a year of being on high alert the court official recalled his spies.

Storm the Fortress

One night, a year and a half after Naganori's death, the 47 rōnin attacked Yoshinaka's mansion. Splitting into two groups, they took the fortress by stealth, killing any retainer who stood in their way, until they found Yoshinaka's bedroom. Here, Yoshinaka was afforded the same right as Naganori: to commit suicide by seppuku. But Yoshinaka could not go through with it. Instead he was beheaded by Yoshio,

who lay the head on Naganori's grave before the whole group of rōnin turned themselves over to the Shōgun. This presented the Shōgun with something of a quandary. On one hand, the rōnin had acted with absolute honour according to the precepts of bushidō. On the other hand, the rōnin had assassinated a member of the Shōgun's entourage after he had ordered that Naganori's death must not be avenged. All 47 rōnin were therefore told to commit seppuku, which they did standing by Naganori's grave in a final act of tribute.

The site soon became a shrine for pilgrims celebrating the rōnin's deeds. One pilgrim was the

Above: A seppuku ceremony shows the moment where the condemned samurai makes the fatal cut, before being beheaded by his second.

Facing page: The 47 Rōnin are confronted on the Ryōgoku Bridge en route to Naganori's grave, following their assassination of Yoshinaka.

Satsuma man who had kicked a drunken Yoshio in the street. In an act of retribution for his callousness, the Satsuma man wept, cried for forgiveness and then committed seppuku on Yoshio's grave.

An epilogue to the story concerns the fate of the rōnins' wives, who also committed the female equivalent of seppuku after hearing of their husbands' deaths. Called jigai, this involved tying the legs together to maintain a dignified pose in death before slicing open the jugular.

Edo Seppuku

After Tokugawa Ieyasu put down his rival Hideyori at Ōsaka Castle and declared there would 'be no more wars', opportunities to commit seppuku as part of samurai warfare naturally decreased. Seppuku, however, became more frequent during the Edo Period. Junshi in particular gained popularity among samurai whose masters had died of natural causes rather than in combat. Ironically, it was also the lack of combat that led directly to the rise in seppuku, not as junshi but as a form of capital punishment.

Forced suicide arose out of Ieyasu's edict of 'no more wars'. His disbanding of the provincial armies made tens of thousands of samurai instantly unemployed, and many were forced to join the already high numbers of rōnin drifting aimlessly around the country. A great deal of troublemaking ensued, as out-of-work samurai became involved in brawling, womanizing, stealing and hiring themselves out as swordsmen. All of these offences were punished in the same way – seppuku. It was

hoped that it would reduce the numbers of samurai misbehaving. For many, however, there was little to live for anyway, and at least seppuku allowed for an honourable exit.

To deal with increasing numbers of seppuku during the Edo Period more attention was paid to its ceremonial aspects. Manuals began to emerge on how to perform a seppuku ceremony, often going into minute details – from the red colour of the mats to prevent staining to the best way to decapitate the seppuku principal. This was the task of a second, a thankless job that only ever raised a stir when it was performed incorrectly. The second would always be blamed if the head flew off and hit officials, or rolled out of sight. For this reason it was suggested that 'for seconds, men are wanted who have distinguished themselves in the military arts. Every samurai should be able to cut off a man's head: therefore, to have to employ a stranger to act as second is to incur the charge of ignorance of the arts of war, and is a bitter mortification.'

The Condemned Man

Up to three seconds were employed for a seppuku ceremony. They would help the condemned samurai dress in a white kimono, eat a final meal and write a death poem. Great emphasis was placed on decorum, and it was recommended that the execution itself took place quickly. 'If in his talk he should express himself like a noble samurai, all pains should be exhausted in carrying out his execution. Yet however careful a man he may be, as he nears his death his usual demeanour will undergo a change.'

Only the bravest samurai would perform a special form of seppuku called jūmonji giri. This was carried out without a second and used a vertical instead of a horizontal cut. The warrior was then expected to hold his hands over his face and remain quiet while he bled to death.

An Historical Account

The act of ceremonial seppuku was still being performed in the mid-nineteenth century, when foreigners entered the country for the first time in over 200 years. Seppuku was the cause of horror and fascination for these visitors, and some dignitaries were even invited to view the ceremony. One such man was Algernon Bertram Freeman-Mitford, a British lord and diplomat during the Meiji Restoration. Mitford wrote an eyewitness account of seppuku, which he said he found shocking at the time, but on his return to Britain sang its praises: 'We in this country are apt to look on hara-kiri as a barbarous and even theatrical form of suicide. It is nothing of the kind. It is indeed the sublimation of all those ideas of honour which constitute the very essence of chivalry.'

Seppuku was abolished along with the samurai not long after Mitford's account, but it continued as a national phenomenon into the twentieth century. Most notably, seppuku was committed by Japanese officers defeated in battle during World War II.

Mitford's description of the seppuku ceremony in his 1871 book *Tales of Old Japan* is one of the few eyewitness accounts and certainly the only one written in English: 'I may here describe an instance of such an execution which I was sent officially to witness. The condemned man was Taki Zenzaburō, an officer of the Prince of Bizen, who gave the order to fire upon the foreign settlement at Hiogo in the month of February 1868… We were invited to follow the Japanese witnesses into the hondo or main hall of the temple, where the ceremony was to be performed. It was an imposing scene. A large hall with a high roof supported by dark pillars of wood. From the ceiling hung a profusion of those huge gilt lamps and ornaments peculiar to Buddhist temples. In front of the high altar, where the floor, covered with beautiful white mats, is raised some three or four inches from the ground, was laid a rug of scarlet felt. Tall candles placed at regular intervals gave out a dim mysterious light, just sufficient to let all the proceedings be seen. The seven Japanese took their places on the left of the raised floor, the seven foreigners on the right. No other person was present.

'After an interval of a few minutes of anxious suspense, Taki Zenzaburō, a stalwart man, 32 years of age, with a noble air, walked into the hall attired in his dress of ceremony, with the peculiar hempen-cloth wings which are worn on great occasions. He was accompanied by a kaishaku [chief second] and three officers… Slowly, and with great dignity, the condemned man mounted on to the raised floor, prostrated himself before the high altar twice, and seated himself on the felt carpet with his back to the high altar, the kaishaku crouching on his left-hand side. One of the three attendant officers then came forward, bearing a stand of the kind used in temples

Left: A samurai wife performs jigai, or female seppuku, which involved cutting the jugular instead of the stomach. The tied legs ensured a dignified pose in death.

The Seppuku Ceremony

Public executions by seppuku were highly ritualized occasions, observed by witnesses. The following protocol for a seppuku ceremony is an abridged version from Kudo Yukihiro's *Records of Suicide by Sword*, translated by A.B. Mitford in 1871.

Preparing the Site

If the execution takes place in a room, white cotton cloth should be laid down and mats prepared. Two screens should be set up to conceal the dirk [wakizashi] upon a tray, a bucket to hold the head after it has been cut off, an incense burner, a pail of water and a basin.

The Sentence

When the sentence has been read, the condemned may say, 'Sirs, I have nothing to say. Yet, since you are so kind as to think of me, I should be obliged if you would deliver such and such a message to such a one.' This is the proper sort of speech for the occasion.

Seconds

The seconds must understand that should there be any mistake they must throw the condemned man, and, holding him down, cut off his head or stab him to death. Three men are employed: the chief second strikes off the head; the assistant second brings forward the tray on which is placed the dirk; the third second carries the head to the chief witness for identification.

The Act

The condemned man should be caused to die as quickly as possible. If the execution is delayed, it will cause the prisoner's courage to fail him. The principal should sit facing the west, the second facing the north. When the principal has taken his place, the second strips his right shoulder of his dress. Then the assistant second brings out the tray on which is laid the dirk. The principal reaches

Left: A form of seppuku called jūmonji was performed without a second and required the condemned man to cover his face with his hands while he bled to death.

out his hand to draw the tray towards him. He then inserts the dirk in the left side of his belly and drags it to the right.

Decapitation

There are three rules for the time of cutting off the head: the first is when the dirk is laid on the tray; the second is when the principal looks at the left side of his belly before inserting the dirk; the third is when he inserts the dirk. Then the blow should be struck without delay. Should he take bad aim and cut the shoulder by mistake, and should the principal rise and cry out, before he has time to writhe, he should hold him down and stab him to death, and then cut off his head. If the body does not fall at once, the second should pull the feet to make it fall. There are some who say that the perfect way to cut off the head is not to cut right through the neck at a blow, but to leave a little uncut, and, as the head hangs by the skin, to seize the top-knot and slice it off.

The Head

When the head has fallen, the second should take out paper from the bosom of his dress and taking the top-knot of hair in his right hand, should lay the head upon the paper, and submit it for inspection. When the identification of the head is concluded, the second places it in a bucket and the ceremony is concluded.

Above: Diplomat Algernon Bertram Freeman-Mitford was the only Englishman to record an account of seppuku. Here, he is satirised in another role as Office of Works Secretary.

for offerings, on which, wrapped in paper, lay the wakizashi, the short sword or dirk of the Japanese, nine inches and a half in length, with a point and an edge as sharp as a razor's. This he handed, prostrating himself, to the condemned man, who received it reverently, raising it to his head with both hands, and placed it in front of himself.

'After another profound obeisance, Taki Zenzaburō, in a voice which betrayed just so much

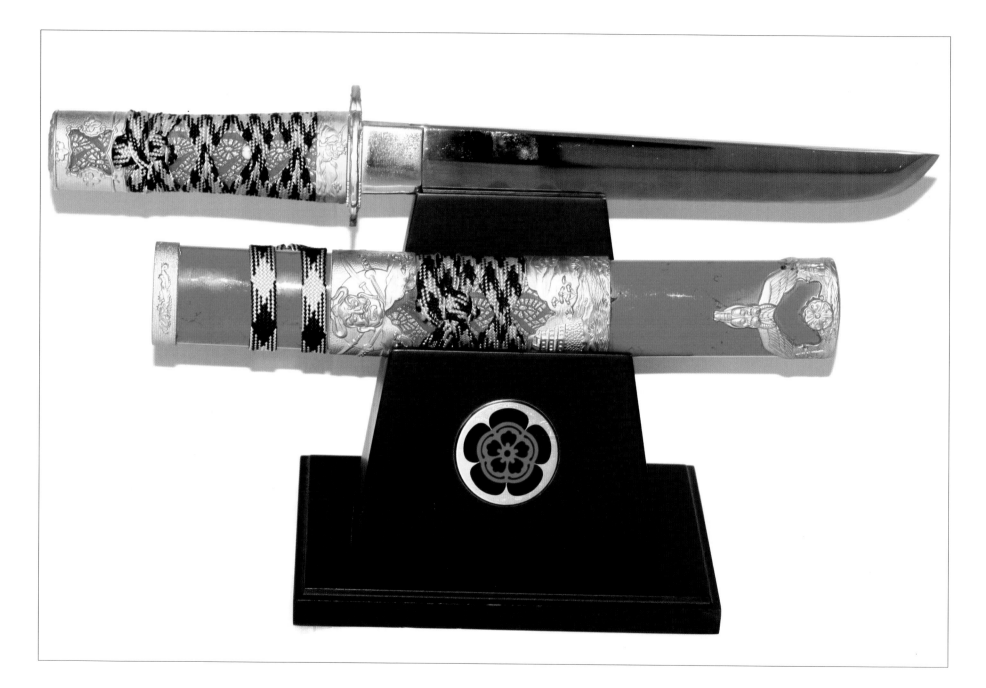

emotion and hesitation as might be expected from a man who is making a painful confession, but with no sign of either in his face or manner, spoke as follows: "I, and I alone, unwarrantably gave the order to fire on the foreigners at Kōbe, and again as they tried to escape. For this crime I disembowel myself, and I beg you who are present to do me the honour of witnessing the act."

'Bowing once more, the speaker allowed his upper garments to slip down to his girdle, and remained naked to the waist. Carefully, according to custom, he tucked his sleeves under his knees to prevent himself from falling backwards; for a noble Japanese gentleman should die falling forwards. Deliberately, with a steady hand, he took the dirk that lay before him; he looked at it wistfully, almost affectionately; for a moment he seemed to collect his thoughts for the last time, and then stabbing himself deeply below the waist on the left-hand side, he drew the dirk slowly across to the right side, and, turning it in the wound, gave a slight cut upwards. During this sickeningly painful operation he never moved a muscle of his face. When he drew out the dirk, he leaned forward and stretched out his neck; an expression of pain for the first time crossed his face, but he uttered no sound. At that moment the kaishaku, who, still crouching by his side, had been keenly watching his every movement, sprang to his feet, poised his sword for a second in the air; there was a flash, a heavy, ugly thud, a crashing fall; with one blow the head had been severed from the body.

'A dead silence followed, broken only by the

hideous noise of the blood throbbing out of the inert heap before us, which but a moment before had been a brave and chivalrous man. It was horrible. The kaishaku made a low bow, wiped his sword with a piece of paper which he had ready for the purpose, and retired from the raised floor; and the stained dirk was solemnly borne away, a bloody proof of the execution.

'The two representatives of the Mikado then left their places, and, crossing over to where the foreign witnesses sat, called us to witness that the sentence of death upon Taki Zenzaburō had been faithfully carried out. The ceremony being at an end, we left the temple.'

Tales of Old Japan, A.B. Mitford, 1871.

Above: A.B. Mitford was a foreign dignitary invited to a seppuku ceremony. His account recalled the 'hideous noise of the blood throbbing out of the inert heap before us'.

Facing page: A ceremonial seppuku dagger, which was laid out on a tray in front of the condemned samurai by one of his seconds.

Samurai Social Structure

The samurai social structure, and the rise and demise of the feudal system, is a story of the warriors' struggle for power that spans the entire length of their history. During that time, samurai clans would clash for domination of the country and establish systems to codify their rule.

Early on, they would achieve control over the Emperor through the Shōgunate, a military government originally designed to protect him against barbarians. Later, during the heyday of the samurai in the late sixteenth century, the warriors would install a four-tiered feudal system that put themselves at the top and merchants at the bottom. Falling outside of this system were the untouchables: criminals, prostitutes and actors, and the Emperor himself – the divine ruler who occupied a pinnacle far above class boundaries.

The story of the samurai's social structure is one that begins and ends with the Emperor. It is

Facing page: Bustling metropolises developed during the Edo Period of peace and offered entertainments such as kabuki theatre, tea houses and brothels.

Right: This scroll depicts the Ainu, the indigenous people of Japan. Their descendants, the Emishi, were the 'barbarians' the samurai were first charged with subduing.

perhaps odd, in that case, that at best he plays only a supporting role. Although the Emperor had been chosen according to a 'mandate from heaven', any real power was soon wrested from his grasp by the very people he had hired to serve him – the samurai. But eventually, after seven centuries of samurai control, the Emperor would once again reign supreme as the warriors' power faded and Japan was forced into the modern world.

Samurai Ascension

The very first Japanese warriors were charged with protecting the Emperor against indigenous 'barbarians' and those who rebelled against his rule. They were led by a 'Shōgun', or 'barbarian-subduing commander in chief', a position instigated by Emperor Sujin sometime between 97 and 30 BC. Back then, the position of Shōgun was a temporary commission during turbulent times. The warriors he led were not samurai – no such class existed at that time. Instead

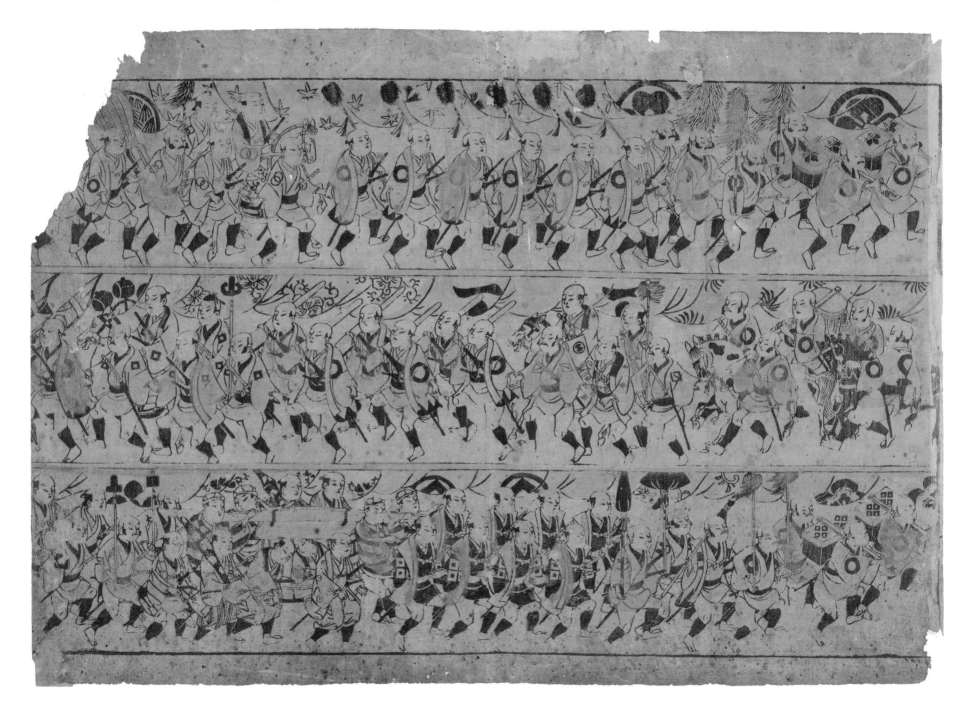

they were men of fighting age expected to serve the Emperor. Among their number were peasants who could wield a spear or rake.

It was the Emishi, descendents of the indigenous Japanese Ainu, that the Emperor's warriors were tasked with subduing. The Emishi were tough hill-people who fought at close quarters on horseback with bows and arrows. They also carried a sword with a curved slashing blade. These fighting methods astonished the imperial warriors who carried a Chinese straight sword and fought in regimented lines. The warriors were often defeated by the Emishi, and had to adapt to this new threat. They used the sincerest form of military flattery: imitation. It is perhaps ironic that battle lessons from the Emishi 'barbarians' went on to form the basis of the fighting techniques employed by the Japanese martial elite that followed – the samurai.

By the tenth century, the warriors protecting the imperial borders often belonged to the clans occupying the provinces closest to the hotspots. These were usually at the outer reaches of the empire, away from the imperial court at Kyoto. Kyoto was believed to be the cultural hub of the civilized world, and many courtiers and nobles found it unthinkable that there could be a worthwhile life outside it. However, the great numbers of courtly nobles and aristocrats without jobs were a great burden on the capital's coffers. As a result, many courtiers were banished to the provinces and given new surnames. Two of the most famous were the Minamoto and the Taira.

The provinces were soon replete with dispossessed nobles and aristocrats who became wealthy landowners and heads of powerful clans. Beneath the landowners were farmers and small landholders who paid them rent and dividends. But over time the relationship became more than financial – bonds were formed, often through inter-marriage, and a quasi-feudal structure was

Above: The Minamoto and Taira were the two most powerful clans in twelfth century Japan. They came to blows in the 1180–1185 Gempei War.

Facing page: A long procession of nobles and courtiers march through Kyōto. Many members of Kyōto's aristocracy were forced out of the capital in the tenth century.

Right: Hōjō Yasutoki was the third regent of the Hōjō Shōgunate. Under the Hōjō, an early feudal system began to emerge.

created. At the top was the 'master' landowner, usually of royal lineage. Underneath him was the 'samurai', or 'one who serves'. As this new samurai class grew more powerful, the term 'daimyō' was

Feudal Beginnings

The Kamakura Period was the age when a feudal system in Japan first began to take shape. Large private estates called shōen were owned by the aristocracy, the Emperor or the temples, and were managed by resident samurai landlords. These landlords supervised the local villages and the production of rice. They built themselves large estate houses. Some landlords were directly accountable to the aristocrat or temple owners, while others became vassals of the Shōgun. This meant they performed military duties for him and in return received a share of land confiscated in war. But problems occurred when samurai landlords wanted to extend their control over the local peasants and farmers, and to improve their share of the profits from the land. At that time there was a hierarchy among the peasantry. At the top was the farmer with taxable fields and below was the 'genin', or 'low person', who worked as a labourer or servant.

used to describe military landowners who exercised territorial control over the clan domains into which the country had been divided.

It would not take long for the clans to begin a power struggle that would continue between samurai houses until the late sixteenth century. In the twelfth century, the two clans at the top were the Minamoto and the Taira, and their clashes would culminate in the epic 1180–85 Gempei War. The climax of the Gempei War was the sea battle of Dannoura, when the defeated Taira survivors committed mass seppuku, many of them weighing down their bodies and drowning themselves. After the war, Minamoto Yoritomo was given the post of Shōgun by the teenage Emperor Go-Toba. This would usher in a new age where Japan was controlled exclusively by the samurai. For the next 750 years Japan's Emperors would have only theoretical authority and instead were the puppet of the real ruler, the Shōgun.

But Minamoto control would not last. Instead, it would be supplanted by the Hōjō – the clan responsible for holding off two Mongol invasions in the thirteenth century, with the aid of a devastating typhoon known afterwards as kamikaze, or 'wind of the gods'. The Hōjō's reign would usher in the Kamakura Period, named after the clan's capital.

After only a century or so the Hōjō's star was on the wane. When it hit its lowest point the Hōjō government suffered an internal coup led by Emperor Go-Daigo, who had ambitions to reinstate imperial power. But once the Hōjō were overthrown, Go-Daigo infuriated his supporters among the Ashikaga samurai by deciding not to award them the Shōgunate. So they marched on Kyoto and took it instead. In the end, the sum total of Go-Daigo's efforts was to replace one Shōgun with another, keeping the power of the Emperor firmly in the pocket of the Shōgunate. When Go-Daigo fled Kyoto to rule as Emperor from the south, the Ashikaga simply installed their own Emperor in the capital. The period of 'The Wars Between the Courts' began. In the end the Ashikaga would be victorious, although their grip on power became as tenuous as that of the Emperor above them as the country entered the Sengoku Jidai, or 'The Age of the Country at War'.

Land Disputes

During the Sengoku Jidai, daimyōs sought to enlarge their domains by seizing territories from neighbouring daimyō. But a daimyō's control over his own province was also brought into question by the social mobilization of the peasants, who were starting to resist their landlords.

Below: Emperor Go-Daigo had ambitions to seize control from the Shōgun and reinstate imperial power. His coup instead ended in a two-emperor system.

This new movement involved the rise of the genin, or 'low person', and was called 'gekokujō', or 'the low overcomes the high'. Many peasants took action against oppressive landlords, marching out of their rice paddies and forming leagues of commoner warriors called Ikki. Some of the Ikki went on to form a group called the Ikkō-ikki, who overthrew the samurai clan of the Kaga province and ruled in the daimyō's stead.

The Ikkō-ikki became a thorn in the side of Oda Nobunaga, another that took advantage of the age of gekokujō by rising through the ranks to become daimyō. After conquering the territory of other daimyō, Nobunaga strengthened his control by dividing Oda provinces among his own generals. He then instigated land surveys within this territory to assess the level of taxation and obligation each landowner owed him. As Nobunaga expanded his domains through his policy of conquest and unification, those generals who helped him received landholdings among the confiscated territory. But while these new landowners were free to exploit the land for personal profit, it was made clear to them that they were Nobunaga's vassals, and he would have the final say over the land.

In addition to his own cadastral surveys, Nobunaga also registered the land of the temples. This was a controversial move that alienated Nobunaga from the country's most powerful religious orders. No-one, not an Emperor or Shōgun, had ever requested a survey of a temple's holdings. Those temples that complied had no further problems with the daimyō, but those that refused were met with force. By the time of his death Nobunaga's social policy was following feudal lines, with powerful daimyō allies at the top, their vassals below followed by those who worked for them. It was a structure that made a clear division between samurai and everyone else in society, a policy that would be consolidated by Toyotomi Hideyoshi.

Hideyoshi was the ultimate gekokujō samurai success story. Born a peasant, he worked as sandal-bearer and made his way up through the samurai ranks to become a daimyō. His metamorphosis was made complete in 1591 when he assumed the title of Taikō, or chancellor. As a genin, Hideyoshi did not have the royal lineage to become Shōgun, and his social policies ensured that no other genin could rise through the ranks as he had done. At the heart of Hideyoshi's unification of Japan was the separation of warriors and peasants. In effect, this abolished the very concept of gekokujō.

To achieve this goal, Hideyoshi adopted issued a series of edicts, the first of which made it illegal for anybody except the samurai to carry arms. The edict's intention, spelt out in black and white, was to define Japan along feudal lines. Samurai warriors would be at the top of this new social order, and their badge of privilege were their swords. Underneath them were the peasants, who until this point had picked up arms when necessary to fight on behalf of their domain. The edict was not only a terrible humiliation for the peasants, it also ensured they could not arm themselves to do anything about it.

Social Divisions

Hideyoshi's next law, commonly known as the 'Separation Edict', built upon the first by classifying three orders – samurai, peasants and townsmen (merchants and artisans) – and making movement between them illegal. In addition, the edict required the inhabitants of towns and villages to watch one another closely and subject any stranger to rigorous examination. Failure to uphold any of the clauses in the edict resulted in individual or collective punishment by force.

Above: Merchants were at the bottom of the four tier social system of feudal Japan. Despite this, the merchants were usually wealthier than their samurai betters.

Facing page: From his residence at Gifu, Oda Nobunaga ordered a survey of every temple's holdings. No such request had ever been made of the country's religious orders.

The Separation Edict

1. If there should be living among you any formerly in military service who have taken up the life of a peasant since the seventh month of last year, since the end of the campaign in Oshu, you are hereby authorized to take them under surveillance and expel them. If persons of their type are kept concealed in any place, the entire town or village shall be brought to justice for this evasion of the law.

2. If any peasant abandons his fields, either to pursue trade or to become a tradesman or labourer for hire, not only shall he be punished but the entire village should be brought to judgement. Anyone who is not employed either in military service or in cultivating land shall likewise be investigated by the local authorities and expelled. If local officials fail to take action in such cases, they shall be stripped of their posts for negligence and their investitures confiscated. In cases involving concealment of peasants who have turned to trade, the entire village, town or neighbourhood shall be held accountable for the offence.

3. No military retainer who has left his master without permission, whether he be samurai or komono [samurai servants] shall be given employment by another. A thorough investigation should be made of the man's previous status and he should be required to provide a guarantor. Those who fail to report that they already have a master are to be arrested for violating the law and returned to their former master. If you violate these laws and permit such a person to go free, three heads shall be cut off and dispatched to the previous master in place of that one man's head. If restitution is not made in this manner, there will be no alternative except to hold the new master responsible and bring him to justice without inquiries into the merits of the case.

Vermillion seal of Hideyoshi

Hideyoshi's separation edict notably did not mention the residents of towns, as it was the Taikō's policy to encourage urban expansion and the merchants and artisans trading within them were of no threat. However, a new law in 1592 made it compulsory for daimyō to 'register in each place, the military men as military men, the farmers as farmers and the townsmen as townsmen.' Movement of these classes between provinces was forbidden. While peasants were now required to stay in the villages, the 'townsmen', the merchants and artisans, were forbidden from moving to the villages and instead had to live in the towns. The samurai were forced to leave the villages for barrack life in one of their daimyō's castle towns.

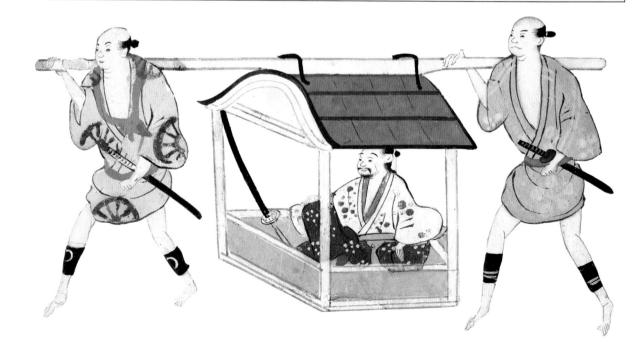

In these towns, the samurai's distinction as the higher caste of Japanese society was made explicit. In addition to the wearing of swords, Hideyoshi required samurai to don richer robes than the commoners, with kimonos that had silk lining. The location of homes within castle towns, the privilege of eating white rice and special hairstyles were other examples of the class divisions. Now that the samurai were away from their native villages, they were completely dependent on their daimyō. This was a beneficial arrangement for the daimyō: his warriors were on hand and battle-ready should they be needed, and the villages, which supplied the rice and taxes, did not have the arms to organize resistance against him.

The Land Survey

Between 1583 and 1598, Hideyoshi developed a comprehensive land survey of the unified domains of Japan. The survey was designed to register each province's wealth by assessing the quantity of its rice produce in a system called kokudaka. A koku represented the amount of rice one person would consume in a year, which equalled around five bushels. Rice provided an easily understandable

Facing page: Under Toyotomi Hideyoshi's Separation Edict, samurai were entitled to carry swords, wear expensive clothes and travel by palanquin.

taxation method and was a practical form of currency. Large amounts of rice were needed as the staple diet of the samurai now in residence with their respective daimyōs. This rice would be provided by the peasants, now officially in a class below the samurai, as a tax on their land. The amount of tax depended on the number of the fields and the size of the rice output, now all neatly registered as part of Hideyoshi's survey. Rice taxes were high: even in the event of a natural disaster

destroying a peasant's crops, they would still be required to present two-thirds of their harvest to the daimyō, with only one-third for themselves. Peasants had little means of improving their lot as Hideyoshi's legislation forbade them from neglecting their fields or moving elsewhere. This often placed peasants in a hopeless situation when a harvest failed. Faced with a choice between starvation or the punishment of death for breaking the rules, many peasants took the risk and absconded.

The Four Tiers of Feudal Japan

Some fell outside of the four tiers. At the top end, they included the Emperor, followed by the Shōgun and the priests. Falling below the class system altogether were Japan's outcasts known as Burakumin. These included occupations considered impure, such as undertakers, butchers, executioners and tanners. Other outcasts were actors, prostitutes, geisha, bards, criminals and the indigenous Ainu people.

THE SAMURAI

Samurai made up around six per cent of the population and were at the top of the social tree. They were paid a stipend of rice and lived in and around their daimyō's castle. This led to the creation of castle towns that in time would become thriving metropolises.

PEASANTS

Making up around 80 per cent of the population, peasants were considered to have an honourable occupation as they produced the rice on which the country depended. Despite this, heavy taxation meant they could not always afford to consume any of the rice they produced. Instead they often survived on millet.

ARTISANS

Part of the 'townsmen' mentioned in Hideyoshi's ordinances, artisans occupied their own sector of towns and cities. Here, they produced goods such as clothes, tools, crockery and samurai swords.

Above: Life in the peasant villages became increasingly controlled under Hideyoshi. Neighbours were encouraged to spy on each other.

MERCHANTS

Travelling merchants and shopkeepers were the lowest rung of samurai society because they generated wealth from the labour of others, such as the artisans. Like the artisans, merchants occupied a separate part of towns and cities, usually considered the least desirable neighbourhoods.

The result of Hideyoshi's edicts, his land survey and various other ordinances was a feudal system based on kokudaka assessment. Provincial daimyō submitted to Hideyoshi's regime as his vassals, which replaced the earlier alliance-led relationship they had enjoyed with Nobunaga. Now Japan had a four-tiered class system that positioned the samurai firmly at the top.

Samurai Society

When Tokugawa Ieyasu came to power he reinforced the feudal system created by Oda Nobunaga and Hideyoshi Toyotomi. His most pressing problem was to maintain control of the country's daimyō under his central power. To do this, he gave landholdings to the daimyō who had been loyal to him at the Battle of Sekigahara and the Siege of Osaka, and made life difficult for those that had opposed him. Daimyō were accordingly classed by their relationship to the Shōgun: Shimpan (kinsmen); Fudai (hereditary vassals); and Tozama (outsiders whom the Shōgun distrusted). All daimyō were bound to the Shōgun by oath and were forced to adopt his law and bureaucratic systems. In its simplest terms, Ieyasu ruled by treating his daimyō as though they were servants looking after Tokugawa property on his behalf. In return for this privilege, the daimyō would have to provide military services to the Shōgun. To maintain control, Ieyasu adopted a tight, hierarchical social structure so that everyone would know their place and what was expected of them. The daimyō's vassal-lord relationship with the

Left: The correct protocol for commoners during a samurai procession was to move to the side of the road and bow their heads.

Shōgun would be replicated within each daimyō's clan on a smaller scale.

At the start of the Tokugawa Shōgunate there were around 200 daimyō in Japan. The title daimyō assumed a formal definition under Ieyasu, meaning a landowner with an annual income of 10,000 koku or more. From his koku, the daimyō would then pay his samurai a rice stipend, the amount based on their importance within the social strata. From the time of Ieyasu's reign, samurai of many occupations other than the military made up the samurai caste. For each daimyō, this was a necessary part of running his domain and the number of samurai working for him each had a different role.

Role of the Samurai

A daimyō's top-level samurai such as his council of elders had direct access to the daimyō and could accrue enough personal wealth to retain their own samurai vassals. These top-level samurai were responsible for the domain's policies and supervising the next level of officials, who were mainly military heads and bureaucrats. Their roles included administration of the castle town and outlying rural areas, finance and the collection and allocation of koku, public works, education, religious affairs and so on. Low-level samurai had jobs such as guards, clerks and messengers who were badly paid and had little chance to improve themselves. Those outside the social structure of the daimyō's samurai were the rōnin, masterless warriors who drifted from place to place to duel, gamble and act as swords for hire or fall into banditry.

Above: Many samurai became rōnin during the Edo Period. Being a rōnin was considered a miserable existence that was to be avoided at all costs.

Becoming a rōnin was considered a fate little better than death. It meant a warrior was left without a clan to support him or a daimyō to pay his stipend of rice. Often samurai were made rōnin when their lord died without leaving an heir, but they could also be made rōnin as punishment or even for committing a petty crime such as brawling. The threat of being made a rōnin kept most samurai in line. The majority were concerned with managing their own lives and living off whatever stipend was paid to them. For military heads, their stipend was used to pay any warriors in his service. This could include anything from a few retainers to a whole garrison.

Samurai in a daimyō's garrison lived in a range of dwellings in and around the castle. Some shared barracks and others had their own houses for wives and children. At the lower end, a married samurai's home could be living quarters within a large building; at the upper end it could be a large detached house, depending on the samurai's rank. Wives took care of household duties including all purchasing, as handling cash was not deemed fitting for a samurai. As well as being wives and daughters, samurai women were still a part of the martial order and expected to fight if necessary. Women therefore carried a dagger in their belt sash and many were trained to use a naginata. The naginata had been the traditional weapon of the samurai woman for several centuries. It was expected that samurai women would make a last defensive line in the home if a village or town was invaded by enemy warriors. This actually happened at the 1333 Battle of Kamakura, when forces loyal to

Life at the Top

Castle life for those at the top was a far cry from that experienced by the samurai in a daimyō's garrison. The three unifiers, Nobunaga, Hideyoshi and Ieyasu, all built lavish castles that reflected their status and egomania. These massive stone structures, adorned with ramparts and surrounded by moats, served the practical purpose of deterring invaders. The interiors were ostentatiously designed in styles most pleasing to their owner. Hideyoshi's Momoyama Castle featured large screens, sliding doors and richly-painted pictures of animals and landscapes in gold leaf. Hideyoshi also constructed large rooms for tea ceremonies, an event that could span several days. The Taikō was said to spend fortunes on fine tea bowls and caddies for his ceremonies. Hideyoshi also spent considerable sums as patron to tea master Sen no Rikyū, the man responsible for bringing the ceremony to the forefront of Japanese consciousness and turning it into a cultural event. Hideyoshi later changed his mind about Rikyū and ordered him to commit seppuku.

Above: A twentieth century replica of Toyotomi Hideyoshi's lavish Momoyama Castle.

Left: An Edo Period tea bowl. Hideyoshi would spend extravagantly on his tea ceremonies.

Emperor Go-Daigo overran the Hōjō capital of Kamakura and put it to the sword. But in this case not even a last bastion of samurai women armed with naginatas could stop the onslaught, and the inhabitants of Kamakura committed mass seppuku.

Unmarried and low-level samurai, such as ashigaru, lived together in barrack buildings. When not on duty, they would spend their time gambling, smoking pipe tobacco, wrestling and playing music or writing poetry. The arts were heavily encouraged during Ieysau's later years, mostly as a diversion from fighting. Interestingly, the extent of a clan's participation in such cultivated pastimes often depended largely on its own history, and whether its lineage could be traced back to aristocracy. Even in the twelfth century, the Taira were considered a cultured and civilized clan whose attention to the arts brought style and refinement to an otherwise coarse and uncouth provincial world. Their rivals in the provinces, the Minamoto, had by comparison a reputation for being vulgar philistines. In the sixteenth and seventeenth centuries, some of the newer clans also despised pastimes that were not bound up in the martial ethos and could make a warrior 'soft'. Daimyō Katō Kiyomasa suggested that if any samurai wanted a 'diversion' it should be an outdoor pursuit such as falconry or deer hunting. Under Kiyomasa, Noh Drama was forbidden and any warrior who took an interest in dancing would be forced to commit seppuku. It is probably fair to say the artistic pursuits of most early Tokugawa ashigaru were mainly writing three-line haiku poems. These were akin to an Irish limerick, with a coarse subject to amuse the men.

Left: A high-ranking samurai wife wields a naginata. Once used by samurai women to defend their homes, naginatas took an increasingly ceremonial role during the Edo Period.

Facing page: This boar hunt screen was presented to King William III of the Netherlands in 1860 by Shōgun Tokugawa Iemochi.

'No More Wars'

When his power over the daimyōs was complete, Ieyasu set out in law a number of reforms to consolidate his control over the rest of the country. The *Kuge Shohatto* (laws for imperial and court officials) was aimed at the Japanese nobility, restricting them to a purely ceremonial role that gave them no power over appointments. In effect,

this prevented the court having any say over the administration of the country. Part of Ieyasu's policy of supremacy over Toyotomi Hideyori at the Siege of Ōsaka was to use a favourite catchphrase: 'no more wars'. This may have confused the many samurai who had been sent from their villages to become a battle-ready garrison at their daimyō's castle town. So, if there were to be 'no more wars',

how were the samurai to spend their time?

Ieyasu's answer was his *Buke Shohatto* (laws for the military houses), a document that laid out a series of ideals on how samurai should behave and what should interest them. These ideas were not new – some of the clauses appeared to be lifted directly from the *Kemmu Shikimoku*, a 1336 Shōgunal code that said 'frugality must

Tokugawa Military Structure

During the Tokugawa period, the military structure of the Shōgunate became more bureaucratic and hierarchical. Each layer could assume some power and autonomy, although it was also strictly controlled under the terms of the vassal-lord relationship. This was to ensure that the rice supplied by the peasants would sustain the costs of keeping standing armies at the ready. The following titles relate specifically to the officer positions of the Tokugawa Shōgunate:

SHŌGUN
The commander-in-chief of Japan.

DAIMYŌ
A landowning warlord who ruled over a domain and had an income of 10,000 koku or more.

HATAMOTO
'Bannermen' who were responsible for forming an army in times of war. The size of the army depended on the hatamoto's income, which was somewhere between 100 and 10,000 koku. As a rough estimate, 1000 koku would cover the cost of two horsemen and 20 ashigaru.

Right: A 1875 triptych of the Edo Period Tokugawa Shōguns. In the foreground is Tokugawa Tsunayoshi, whose animal protection law stopped anyone harming stray dogs.

GOKENIN
Gokenin or 'housemen' were the vassals directly underneath the hatamoto. One of the greatest differences between them was that a gokenin could not seek an audience with the Shōgun, and was paid a smaller income of around 100 koku.

OBAN-GASHIRA
These were the captains of the 'Great Guard', the elite of the Tokugawa fighting force. In addition to the Great Guard, there was a bodyguard to guard the Shōgun, an Inner Guard to guard Edo Castle and units of horsemen and ashigaru that otherwise made up the ranks.

Above: Here, Nijō Castle features the daily life typical of a seventeenth century castle town. Tokugawa Ieyasu ordered Nijō built and paid for by his daimyōs.

Right: Tokugawa Iemitsu was the Shōgun who issued Japan's Sakoku, or 'locked country' policy. No foreigners would be allowed in for over 200 years.

Facing page: Duelling rōnin became such a problem in the Edo Period that a law was passed to punish both participants equally, regardless of who started the duel.

be universally practiced' and that 'drinking and wild frolicking in groups must be suppressed.' Nonetheless, the *Buke Shohatto* would pave the way for a new samurai ethos, known as bushidō, or 'Way of the Warrior'. This would encourage participation in the arts, tea ceremonies, poetry and other cultural pursuits. Ieyasu's thinking was to replace the revolutionary concepts of gekokujō – which had brought him and his predecessors into positions of ultimate power – with the Confucian ideal of kenshin, meaning devotion and loyalty. Samurai, then, were to remain a military order, but one that could replace hand-to-hand combat with martial arts training, the battlefield with calligraphy. The martial successes of great heroes past would be revered and celebrated, as long as no new fighting took place.

In response to their new social position as theoretical warriors, samurai set up schools around the country to teach Kendō, 'The Way of the Sword'. There were certainly enough unemployed samurai to take up jobs as Kendō teachers. As the Tokugawa period progressed, the ranks of rōnin swelled. This was partly because Ieyasu had disbanded many of the provincial clans, particularly those led by Tozama daimyō.

A Peasant's Lot

A common perception among the samurai class was that peasants were like sesame seeds – the harder you squeezed the more you could extract. Life for peasants became increasingly bleak as the Tokugawa Shōguns passed more and more laws to restrict and regulate their lives. Detailed land surveys were issued to extract the greatest amount of rice possible. Tokugawa villages were composed of a group of farmers called hyakushō, each with a small parcel of land. The village hyakushō were required to form into associations of five households, called gonin-gumi, which assumed collective responsibility for tax payments, made sure no local laws were broken and kept an eye on one another.

Enforcing the laws in each village was a group of officers. As well as paying rice taxes, peasants were also taxed on doors, windows, daughters, cloth, sake and beans. In addition to tending their fields, peasants were also expected to help maintain roads, bridges and horse stations. Restrictions were placed on what they could wear and eat, where they could live and sometimes what hours they worked. Buying, selling or abandoning their land was strictly prohibited, as was taking up a different occupation. Despite this latter rule, many peasants fled to find work in burgeoning cities such as Edo or grew crops to sell on the side at markets.

Duelling Samurai

A favourite pastime of travelling rōnin was to challenge the head of a sword-fighting school to a duel. A victorious rōnin could gain great esteem through his efforts, and a defeated teacher could lose his job as well as his life. The samurai duelling, brawling and general troublemaking got so out of hand during this period that several laws had to be passed to prevent it. One such law, called kenka ryoseihai, decreed that both parties in a dispute would be punished equally, regardless of the nature of the dispute and who was responsible for it. The punishment itself was often seppuku. A verdict of seppuku would also be meted out to any samurai involved in petty theft, embezzlement, womanizing, insulting a lord and harbouring Christians.

There was no place for Christians in the samurai's new social order. Their position in society had been tenuous since hordes of disaffected followers joined with Toyotomi Hideyori against Tokugawa Ieyasu at the Siege of Ōsaka. Ieyasu's Christian Expulsion Edict had banned Christians, and Ieyasu's heirs Hidetada and Iemitsu persecuted them even further. For Iemitsu, Christian ideals brought to Japan by colonizing European missionaries had done nothing but damage. His attitude was strengthened when a 1637 uprising by Christians, peasants and rōnin of Kyūshū's Shimabara Peninsula took five months to subdue. Following this uprising Iemitsu passed legislation to root out any secret Christians by forcing all Japanese to register at Buddhist temples. Those registering

Facing page: During Shōgun Iemitsu's reign, daimyōs were forced to split their time between addresses in their domain and Edo. They were often on the road.

were made to trample an image of Christ or the Virgin Mary.

Next, as a measure to counter the perceived threat of foreign influence, Iemitsu issued a series of edicts between 1633 and 1639 making it illegal for any foreigner to enter Japan or any Japanese person to leave. All foreigners, even those Japanese with some foreign blood, were immediately expelled. Japan officially became Sakoku, a 'locked country', and from 1640 its doors were closed to outsiders. The social effect of this policy was to lock Japan into its feudal system for more than 200 years.

The main problem for the samurai during this time was to stay solvent. As the years passed, the cost of living went up but samurai rice stipends stayed the same. Many hatamoto struggled to pay their armed retainers – and the retainers, in turn, could often not meet their own costs. The upkeep on armour, horse fodder, firewood, food and all the other necessities of a samurai existence meant many had to borrow from moneylenders or pawn their possessions. Samurai from the lower-ranks sometimes sold their swords and instead borrowed weapons from friends when they had to perform military duties. Many took part-time jobs, including umbrella-making, teaching and selling bamboo.

While the lower samurai ranks suffered day-to-day, things were not much better at the top

Left: Kabuki theatre was a great Edo Period favourite among city merchants and samurai. This pleasure-seeking urban lifestyle was known as the 'Floating World'.

for the daimyō. Tokugawa Iemitsu had issued an 'Alternate Attendance' law that forced daimyō to divide their time between an address in Edo and one in their native province. Most daimyō had to alternate every year, but those living in the Kanto region had to change addresses every six months. This was deliberately designed to keep daimyō busy travelling and spending large amounts of their revenue so they would never find time to revolt against their Shōgun. The costs incurred by a daimyō travelling to and from Edo with his retinue were enormous, especially given the costs of living in the bustling city.

The Floating World
Edo became a sprawling commercial metropolis in the seventeenth century and was one of the largest cities in the world. Decades of national peace led to the expansion of commerce. Merchants became rich from the sale of cotton, silk and rapeseed oil, and new transport and communication lines were set up to serve their burgeoning trade. Cities such as Edo grew exponentially to support the flow of trade and the needs of the traders themselves. Theatrical districts flourished, as did teahouses and brothels, offering both female and male prostitutes. Fine foods such as cakes and sweets were eaten alongside rice and the traditional arts such as the Noh Drama and flower-arranging flourished. The urban lifestyle

of this period became known as 'the floating world', where increasingly wealthy merchants would mix with samurai at kabuki plays or geisha houses.

This created conflict within Japan's class structure. Merchants occupied the bottom rung of the feudal order, beneath artisans and peasants. There were strict regulations about the way they could behave and what they could wear. This was the source of tension among the merchants themselves, who wished to indulge their increasing financial status with finery and other displays of wealth. Two tiers above the merchants in the social order were the samurai themselves, who were becoming increasingly irrelevant, bitter and financially unable to keep up with the extravagant lifestyles of their feudal inferiors, the merchants.

Closed Door Policy
Despite Japan's obstinate desire to keep its doors shut to the outside world, things were changing within its borders. The policy of separation had frozen the feudal structure with the samurai at the top, but after decades of peace the notion of legions of armed samurai on constant standby for battle was becoming outdated. Instead, actual warfare had been replaced by theories on how it should be conducted. Kendō, the 'Way of the Sword', taught students to fight with blades made of wood and bamboo. Codes such as bushidō and hagakure celebrated heroic deeds of the past and taught how warriors should live and die honorably by the sword. But in the end, the texts only thinly disguised the fact that the samurai had become obsolete.

The situation would come to its logical conclusion in the nineteenth century. By then, the samurai was an upper class trying to eke out a living from the rice stipend paid to them by their social underlings, the peasants. In addition, from the beginning of the new century the Tokugawa Shōgunate had faced peasant uprisings, samurai bankruptcy and increasing demands from foreign powers for Japan to reopen her doors.

When Japan did abandon its closed-door policy, it would set in motion a series of events that sent the Shōgunate spiraling into oblivion. As the Shōgun's power diminished, the samurai turned to one man who could lead them into this new modern age – the Emperor. So it was in 1867 the Shōgun handed back his commission to Emperor Meiji who then took control of the country. Perhaps Emperor Go-Daigo smiled down from the heavens as Meiji finally achieved what he could not – absolute control of Japan under imperial rule. Japan had come full circle, and the power over its future was finally back in the Emperor's grasp.

Above: In 1867 Emperor Meiji took control of Japan. Here Meiji reads out the country's new constitution, which would signal the end for the samurai.

Facing page: By the mid-nineteenth century, Edo was one of the largest cities in the world. In 1868, it was renamed Tokyo and became the imperial capital.

Epilogue: The End of the Samurai

The beginning of the end for the samurai came in the mid nineteenth-century, when foreign ships forced Japan to reopen her doors to outsiders. The Shōgunate policy of Sakoku had served the country for over 200 years, but it was now looking as outdated as the samurai charged with keeping its borders foreigner-free. During that time, dozens of ships from around the world – England, France, Russia, China – had come, tried to land and been told to leave.

Japan was a curiosity to sailing missionaries and merchants with opportunities in mind, and its ports were closest to the best whaling grounds in the world. But these ports remained closed to all except a few Dutch traders, who had obtained a special dispensation from Japan's Sakoku all the way back in the seventeenth century. There was even a sign by the entrance to

Facing page: There would be no question of fighting against a foreign foe whose great guns aboard the 'Black Ships' made all samurai weaponry instantly anachronistic.

Right: Commodore Perry undertook a 'resolute attitude' to his negotiations: if the Shōgun would not end the country's Sakoku policy, Perry would end it for him.

Edo Bay ordering foreign ships to turn around and not come back. Shipwrecked sailors, who did not have the luxury of retreat, were made similarly unwelcome. In 1846 a grounded whaling vessel from New York experienced a Japanese landing committee firsthand. An account by one of the sailors, George Howe, reports the survivors of the wreck walked to the main port on the island of Etorufō:

'As we approached it, we saw what appeared to be a fort. But on coming nearer we found it was a piece of painted cloth extended about three-quarters of a mile, and painted so as to represent a fort with guns. Here, about 60 men armed with swords and spears ran towards us.'

Above: Dutch visitors are pictured visiting Japan in the nineteenth century. Dutch merchants had been allowed to trade with Japan throughout its Sakoku period.

Facing page: Artist William Heine travelled with Commodore Perry to record his Japanese encounters. Here, Perry comes ashore to present his presidential letter to the Shōgun.

Similar canvas forts, measuring a mile long with painted ramparts and cannons, were also constructed when four American warships entered Edo Bay in 1853. Bluffing was the only option open to the samurai on shore, who were left shocked and astounded by these futuristic vessels of war. It was obvious the 'Black Ships' – so called to describe the modernity of their weaponry – would make short work of the Japanese shore batteries armed with seventeenth century cast-iron cannons.

U.S. Naval Supremacy

Leading the black ships was Commodore Matthew C. Perry, whose mission was to open Japan up to American whalers and traders. This was not a tentative request from the Americans. Perry had been studying the country and was well aware of the increasing vulnerability of the samurai. Perry also knew the Shōgun would have to respond to the American's threat of force, and that he also did not have adequate resources to take on his ships. The commodore made his demands clear: he was not interested in dealing with samurai bureaucrats and go-betweens, and instead wanted to deliver a letter from President Millard Fillmore directly to the Emperor himself. With this message Perry included a white flag, so the Japanese had something to fly should they wish to test the mettle of the American guns. While he awaited a response, Perry paraded his ships around the Edo Bay coastline in an

196

Facing page: A Japanese interpretation of Perry's 1854 meeting with a shōgunal official. The Shōgun would reluctantly agree to the Convention of Kanagawa, which gave America trading privileges.

ostentatious show of strength. There were few options open to Shōgun Tokugawa Iemochi. He accepted the letter on the Emperor's behalf and Perry promised to be back in one year's time for his answer: would Japan open her doors or not?

The episode had been a humiliating blow to the Shōgun, who had little choice but to revoke aspects of Japan's Sakoku policy. Despite ordering new batteries and shore fortifications around Edo Bay, Iemochi knew he had no chance of repelling the American ships by force. When Perry returned in 1854, the Shōgun signed the 'Convention of Kanagawa', which gave the Americans access to trade in the faraway ports of Shimoda and Hakodate on Ezo Island. Similar concessions were made for the Russians, whose ships had also made an appearance in 1854. Treaties of the same kind were subsequently made with other nations, including Great Britain.

But the foreign invasion would go further than trade. In 1858, after years of pressured negotiations, the Shōgun signed the Treaty of Amity and Commerce with America. The treaty gave the country access to five Japanese trading ports and allowed for U.S. citizens to live in these ports. It also guaranteed them religious freedom. But the most important aspect of the agreement was the contract's extraterritoriality clause, which meant American citizens living in Japan would be tried under their own judicial system. Similar treaties were also signed with other foreign countries. In effect, this put foreigners above Japanese law, which had been deemed 'very peculiar' by the American who brokered the deal, Townsend Harris. The consequence was that many foreigners adopted an arrogant and superior attitude towards the Japanese.

'Barbarian' Foreigners

The situation was hard for a fiercely independent nation like Japan to tolerate, and created major tensions between the Shōgun, various samurai daimyō and the Emperor himself. Emperor Kōmei even took the remarkable step of calling Shōgun Iemochi to Kyoto to remind him of his position as 'barbarian-subduing commander-in-chief.' Not only had the barbarians not been subdued, they were living on Japanese soil as protected VIPs exempt from Shōgunal law! Samurai daimyō were also unhappy. Some called for a new, more powerful Shōgun to be installed, while others suggested the Emperor himself take back the reins of power. The slogan 'Sonnō jōi', or 'Revere the Emperor! Expel the barbarians!' began to echo around the provinces of Japan. It was only a matter of time before tensions between Japan's martial order and the outsiders would erupt. The flashpoint, which occurred between a party of 'barbarian' foreigners and

Left: Townsend Harris was the American who brokered the 1858 Treaty of Amity and Commerce. The treaty, in effect, put foreigners above Japanese law.

local samurai, showed the growing support for the emperor while at the same time undermining the authority of the Shōgun.

The 'Namamugi Incident' took place in 1862 between Shimazu Hisamitsu, the father of Satsuma daimyō Shimazu Tadayoshi, and Charles Lennox Richardson, a British merchant. Richardson was riding through the Satsuma countryside with three friends when they came upon Hisamitsu and a large procession of his armed retainers. Most Japanese knew the correct protocol in such a situation was to move off the road and bow their heads until the procession had passed. But Richardson, later described by his own uncle as 'reckless and stubborn', decided instead to try and ride through the middle. He was heard to have called back to his party, 'I have been living in China for 14 years, I know how to deal with these people', as he spurred his horse into a gallop. It was an extraordinarily insolent turn that could not stand among the marching samurai. After all, it was still Shōgunal law that a samurai could strike, or even behead, any person who did not show the correct respect. Richardson was surrounded, pulled from his horse and stabbed in ten places. His fellow riders managed to flee to safety.

It was not the first case of trouble between the Japanese and foreigners, but it was the first to become an international incident. Britain demanded reparations for Richardson's murder, and the Shōgun demanded that these came from the Satsuma daimyō himself. The Satsuma samurai refused, instead pointing out that they had been

Left: American foreigners, such as the one pictured, would become a familiar sight from 1858 onwards. But their presence in Japan was far from welcome.

Facing page: In 1863 Emperor Kōmei took the Shōgun to task by issuing a decree that all foreigners be expelled from Japan. The Shōgun ignored the decree.

doing what the Shōgun had not – subduing barbarians on the Emperor's behalf. The British responded by sending a flotilla of warships to shell Kagoshima, the capital of Satsuma. In the ensuing conflict the wooden capital was burned to the ground. Ironically, the British suffered a greater loss of life than those they were shelling, as the samurai returned fire from their outdated cannon batteries. The 11 British dead included the commander of the flagship, HMS *Euryalus*. While both sides claimed victory, the result was actually a stalemate that strangely ended in a business relationship. The Satsuma samurai were so impressed by the British warships that the daimyō decided he wanted his own. Many orders for steamships were subsequently sent to British shipyards, and Satsuma went on to become the hub of the modern Japanese navy.

Above: The British reprisal for the Namamugi Incident was to send warships to shell Kagoshima. Ironically, the British would suffer from heavier casualties than the Japanese.

Facing page: Englishman Charles Lennox Richardson is set upon by Shimazu samurai during the 1862 Namamugi Incident. It was Japan's first modern international incident.

Above: The British Government demanded £25,000 in reparations for Charles Lennox Richardson's murder. Here, Satsuma samurai count the money out.

Facing page: Many Japanese people wanted Shōgun Iemochi to be less of a 'foreign collaborator' and more of a 'subduer of barbarians'. It was an impossible task.

Foreign Threat
The shelling of Kagoshima served to diminish further popular support for the Shōgunate. It had not protected the Satsuma people against the foreigners and instead loaned the daimyō the £25,000 reparation still insisted on by the British government for Richardson's death. There were even rumours that the Shōgunate had offered to send its own steamer to join the British warships. Another

incident saw samurai from the Chōshū province firing on foreign ships in the Shimonoseki Strait. This led to a foreign bombardment of Chōshū's coastal batteries and a severe rebuke from the Shōgun, who sent an army to bring the province under Tokugawa control. Chōshū became a mecca for samurai unhappy with the Shōgun's inaction against the foreigners.

An 1863 decree from Emperor Kōmei that all foreigners be expelled from Japanese shores had been ignored by the Shōgun, but the nature of the request neatly summed up his impossible position. Iemochi did not have the arms to take on the mighty foreign fleets, and he needed the support of these foreign forces to equip and train his men with new modern weaponry. The Shōgun had to bow to the will of the outsiders. The cost of the new weapons combined with a growing bill of reparations for incidents against the outsiders was also weakening the Shōgunate financially. Even so, many of the people of Japan considered the Shōgun to be more of a foreign collaborator than a 'subduer of barbarians'. Every move the Shōgun made appeared to further undermine his rule, while in Kyoto the call of Sonnō jōi became louder and support for the Emperor strengthened.

Kyōto became the gathering-place for crowds of discontented samurai calling for the Shōgun's resignation. Some wanted Iemochi replaced with a more radical Shōgunal alternative from Chōshū or Satsuma – two domains that had openly defied the foreign presence. Others wanted a return to Sakoku, while some wanted to continue modernizing Japan's

weaponry with foreign help. Another large faction sought the abolition of the Shōgunate, with full power returned to the Emperor as head of state. Still more wanted a power-sharing agreement under a unified Shōgunate and an imperial court. The factions often clashed violently. The most notable battles were between Chōshū samurai and the Shinsengumi, a group of rōnin mercenaries originally formed by Iemochi to protect him on his recent imperial visit.

The Shinsengumi quickly became the Kyōto police force and set about arresting samurai factions who supported the Shōgun instead of the Emperor. Those who resisted arrest were killed. Kyōto became something of a Tokugawa police state, where accusations of treachery against the Shōgun were commonplace and plots against his life often exposed. It is hard to determine how many of these 'plots' were real, as the Shinsengumi were a mix of imperial and Shōgunal loyalists and their methods of investigation was often reckless and unreliable. In at least one instance, however, the Shinsengumi did uncover a planned coup against the Shōgun, which was led by a group of Chōshū rōnin. The plotters had apparently intended to set fire to Kyōto but were stopped by the Shinsengumi in a violent showdown known as the Ikedaya Affair.

As a result, all Chōshū samurai were banned from Kyōto by Tokugawa Iemochi, but instead of going quietly the samurai launched an offensive against the Tokugawa samurai guarding the imperial palace. The attack sparked a series of street battles across Kyōto as those loyal to the Emperor clashed with those loyal to the Shōgun. In the end, the Chōshū and their supporters were ousted from the city and a united army made up of Shōgunal and imperial samurai marched against the now common enemy of the state – the Chōshū.

Violence Averted

However, the Kyōto force did not use violence apart from bombarding the Chōshū batteries with the help of friendly foreign ships. Instead a deal for surrender was brokered by Satsuma samurai Saigō Takamori, an imperial loyalist who thought his goals would be better met if he joined forces with his neighbours in Chōshū rather than opposing them. His intervention prevented the Kyōto army and the Chōshū samurai from coming to blows, and also gave those of the Chōshū domain time to prepare themselves for any subsequent attack. Takamori also introduced the Chōshū samurai to Thomas Glover, a Scottish merchant who dealt primarily in the arms trade. Before long, Glover was supplying Chōshū samurai with the weapons needed for modern warfare.

The 1866 Satsuma–Chōshū Alliance, which formed the backbone of the Meiji Restoration, agreed to combine forces should the need arise against a common aggressor. The aggressor in this case was the Tokugawa Shōgun, who was preparing his troops for another march into Chōshū. So the battle lines were drawn – those samurai of the Chōshū and Satsuma domains who were fighting for the restoration of the Emperor, and Tokugawa Iemochi who was

fighting for the existence of the Shōgunate itself. But when Iemochi led an expedition against the Chōshū his men were totally outdone. The Chōshū samurai were carrying modern rifles alongside their swords, and had been trained to use them well. The Satsuma samurai, according to the terms of their Satsuma–Chōshū Alliance, did not come to the Shōgun's aid, but instead stayed on standby, ready to help the Chōshū samurai if needed

The defeat at Chōshū was the last straw for Shōgun Tokugawa Iemochi, who died a couple of weeks later. Emperor Kōmei soon

Left: Thomas Glover was a Scottish merchant who supplied the Satsuma and Chōshū samurai with modern weaponry. He later commissioned warships for the Imperial Japanese Navy.

Facing page: Hijikata Toshizō was one of the commanders of the Shinsengumi, a group of rōnin mercenaries who became the police force of Kyōto.

The Battle of Toba-Fushimi

Above: The four-day Battle of Toba-Fushimi ended in a decisive victory for Emperor Meiji and the Satsuma-Chōshū Alliance.

The four-day Battle of Toba-Fushimi began on 4 January 1868. It pitted the Tokugawa clan and its allies, who included the Kyōto Shinsengumi, against the Satsuma–Chōshū Alliance and its supporters. Both sides carried a hodgepodge of old and new weapons. Some of the Tokugawa samurai had been trained by members of the French military, who had also supplied them with modern rifles. Other members of the Tokugawa side carried only yaris and katanas. Those samurai of the Satsuma–Chōshū Alliance were probably the best equipped, with Armstrong howitzers and Minié rifles.

After two inconclusive initial skirmishes at Toba and Fushimi, news reached Saigō Takamori that Emperor Meiji had declared Tokugawa Yoshinobu to be an enemy of the court. With this message came a set of imperial banners for use by the Satsuma–Chōshū forces. When the banners were unfurled on the final day of battle at Tominomori, they were a decisive blow to the morale of Yoshinobu's men. At first, the Tokugawa did not know what the banners represented and had to send a messenger to the opposing lines to

find out. Once it became clear the Tokugawa were now facing the official Imperial Army its ranks fell into confusion. Upon seeing this, the Satsuma–Chōshū samurai mounted a charge at the Tokugawa lines. To make matters worse, the Tokugawa's allies from the Tsu domain defected to the imperial side and were now firing on Yoshinobu's samurai. The Tokugawa had no choice but to retreat to Ōsaka Castle. From here, Yoshinobu deserted his men under cover of night and fled north.

Facing page: Tokugawa Yoshinobu was the last Shōgun of Japan. He was declared an enemy of the state by Emperor Meiji during the Battle of Toba-Fushimi (above).

followed suit. Iemochi was succeeded by Tokugawa Yoshinobu, the last Shōgun of Japan. Kōmei was succeeded by his son Meiji, the Emperor who would finally wrest control from the Shōgunate after nearly 700 years of its rule.

Yoshinobu's tenure was brief. His appointment had not brought an end to the battles with the Shōgunate, and Yoshinobu realized the only way to avoid a war with the Satsuma–Chōshū Alliance was to resign. Yoshinobu also believed his retirement would open up a new post in a council of samurai daimyō that would act as a new national administration. But he had been duped. The samurai of the Satsuma–Chōshū Alliance had no intention of forming a de facto government, and instead continued to support Meiji as the true ruler of Japan.

Despite this, Yoshinobu continued to behave as though he was still the Shōgun. He commanded large armies, had many allies and held great political sway in Kyōto. While Meiji and his government seemed to accept the long shadow of Yoshinobu, the samurai from the Satsuma and Chōshū domains found his presence intolerable. To end what they saw as the continuing Tokugawa interference with the imperial restoration, Saigō Takamori put pressure on Emperor Meiji to confiscate part of Yoshinobu's lands. Satsuma rōnin set out to further antagonize Yoshinobu by launching a series of terrorist raids in his capital of Edo. Then on the morning of 3 January 1868, Satsuma samurai led by Takamori seized the imperial gates and had Meiji read out a rescript that set out a new plan for Japan under imperial control.

Right: The 1868 Battle of Ueno finished off the last of the Tokugawa retainers, known as the Shōgitai. Here, the battle draws to its bloody conclusion.

Declaration of War

This pushed Yoshinobu into a corner. He ordered a strike against Kyōto to 'free' the Emperor from the influence of the Satsuma–Chōshū Alliance. Oddly, the Tokugawa clan was in effect declaring war on the pro-imperial Satsuma–Chōshū Alliance in the Emperor's name. The conflict became known as the Boshin War, and the armies clashed first on the outskirts of Kyoto in the Battle of Toba-Fushimi.

The outcome of the Battle of Toba-Fushimi did not entirely quell those samurai opposing Emperor Meiji, but it did end his military return to power. His imperial troops easily overthrew Ōsaka Castle and then hunted down the remaining rebels as they headed north. In the end, these last Tokugawa samurai entrenched themselves in the fortress of Goryokaku on Ezo Island, and proclaimed themselves the new 'Republic of Ezo'. The dream lasted for a little while, but the Republic of Ezo was destined to go the same way as the Shōgunate and the samurai.

As part of the Emperor's restoration he moved into Edo Castle and renamed the city Tokyo. From this new Tokyo Imperial Palace, Meiji formed a government made up of those samurai from Satsuma, Chōshū and his court who had supported his restoration. This was the last of the good news for these samurai, as Meiji set about dismantling the feudal system and revoking the privileges of the warrior caste.

Right: A statue of Saigō Takamori and his dog at Ueno Park, Tokyo. Like many of the great samurai heroes, Takamori was tragically fated to lose.

Facing page: Pictured is one of Saigō Takamori's many swordfighting academies, set up after he resigned from Meiji's government. Over 200,000 samurai flocked to join Takamori.

In 1869, Meiji asked the samurai of Satsuma, Chōshū, Tosa and Saga to hand their land to the throne. The rest of the Japanese daimyō were soon told to follow. Then in 1871, the 250 feudal domains were abolished and replaced by 72 prefectures and three metropolitan districts. This left nearly two million samurai without domains to defend, and their ranks were quickly reordered. From 1869, samurai daimyō would be recast as kazoku, or peers; former samurai as shizoku; and everyone else as heimen, or commoners. The kazoku were compensated with European-style titles, such as count, prince and duke, although most would have no real power and none would lead an army of retainers. Instead a new Imperial Army was established and the need for samurai warriors made obsolete. The samurai themselves had their rice stipends revoked and replaced by an annual pension. But like the stipends, these pensions were seldom large enough to cover the cost of living. The final blow was the abolition of the samurai's right to bear arms. The samurai's sword, his badge of identity, privilege and honour, was gone.

The Last Samurai

Saigō Takamori was one of the leaders who watched in horror as the government he had fought to create dismantled the samurai caste piece by piece. He had helped strip the Tokugawa of its land and defeat former Shōgun Yoshinobu at the Battle of Toba-Fushimi.

Now the Shōgunate had been abolished altogether, and Japan looked forward to its new place in a world dominated by technology, modern armaments and, before long, international conflict. But as the country changed from inward-looking backwater to global military power, Takamori would make a stand for those warriors recently made redundant. His rebellion against the Meiji government exemplified all the bushidō qualities of a great samurai, and he went down fighting. His final stand represents the last gasp for feudal Japan and the warriors who ruled over it. For this reason, Saigō Takamori is remembered as a beloved national hero and often known as the last samurai.

Saigō Takamori was not born into the kind of samurai family that promised an auspicious career. His father belonged to the lower ranks of the Satsuma clan that usually worked as the daimyō's bodyguard. After his birth in 1828, Takamori's upbringing was similarly unremarkable.

He was, however, noted for his appearance. Always a big child, by adulthood Takamori had piercing eyes, bushy eyebrows, weighed over 91kg (200lb) and reached 1.8m (6ft) tall – large for a Japanese man at the time. He was considered a popular and honourable warrior who lived by the

Above: Under the Meiji government, the samurai would be replaced by a uniformed imperial army and the city of Tokyo protected by a new police force, pictured.

Above right: The Boshin War effectively brought about the end of the Tokugawa Shogunate's three centuries of rule, re-establishing the power of the Imperial court and the modernizers.

Facing page: Pictured is Saigō Takamori's last stand, at the 24 September Battle of Shiroyama, 1877. His opponents carry the war flag of the Imperial Japanese Army.

tenets of bushidō and rose through the Satsuma samurai ranks quickly.

By his late 30s, Takamori had worked as a Satsuma diplomat in Kyōto and went on to command the domain's samurai stationed there. Takamori hated Shōgun Iemochi, especially after he appeared to side with the foreigners during the

Namamugi Incident that resulted in the British shelling of Kagoshima, Takamori's hometown. After Nagashima, Takamori would do everything in his power to undermine Iemochi. In Kyōto, Takamori was able to meet representatives from other disaffected samurai leaders. But while a skilled swordsman trained in the strategy of war,

鹿児島山争城之戦圖

213

Left: Following Saigō Takamori's demise at Shiroyama, the remaining samurai of the 'Satsuma Rebellion' were forced to surrender to the imperial army.

Takamori was also a canny diplomat. He arranged for the surrender of Chōshū to the Shōgunate in 1865, which prevented an all-out civil war, and at the same time enacted the clandestine Satsuma–Chōshū Alliance. This was an agreement that the Satsuma would join with the samurai of Chōshū if faced with a common aggressor – the Shōgun. The alliance appeared to set in motion Takamori's plans to dispose of the Shōgun and put the Emperor in his place. The Meiji Restoration was short and sharp, and left the Tokugawa in tatters. The Emperor restored to his rightful place, Takamori retired and went home to Kagoshima to watch the new, modern Japan blossom.

Takamori's retirement did not last long. Instead he was persuaded by Emperor Meiji to take command of the new Imperial army of about 10,000 soldiers. With Takamori at the helm, Meiji felt strong enough to make the first devastating blow against the samurai. He announced that the samurai's domains would be broken up and replaced by imperial prefectures, and their armies disbanded. It is perhaps an indication of Takamori's imperial loyalties that he accepted responsibility for this new programme. To help smooth away any conflicted feelings Takamori may have had, the Emperor appointed him Imperial Council of State and promoted him to the rank of general.

Conscription Policy

Now that there were no samurai armies, a debate arose about conscripting troops to the new Imperial Army. As the leading military figure in the country, Takamori was required to respond. The idea of conscription was a major conflict of interests for Takamori. On one hand he saw the modernization of Japan's military as paramount. This had led his campaign against the ineffectual Shōgunate and was the reason he had agreed to become a bureaucrat in Meiji's government. On the other hand, conscription would further undermine the role of the samurai in Japan at a time when the warriors had already been dangerously weakened. In the end, however reluctantly, Takamori advocated conscription into a national army for Japan. But his feelings of loyalty towards the new administration were now changing.

Matters came to a head over Korea, which had refused to recognize Japan's new government and had even turned away three Meiji delegations from its borders. Takamori felt Korea needed to be taught a lesson: an attack would give his army a chance to try its new weaponry as well as giving some unemployed samurai something to do. Takamori suggested he visit Korea and bait the government into killing him, thus giving Japan the excuse it needed to attack. His plan was popular for a time, but in the end it made no sense for Meiji to waste finances on an invasion while Japan was still in the early stages of modernizing its own army.

When news reached Takamori that his plan to invade Korea had been rejected he flew into a rage. He immediately resigned from his post and dozens of his loyal junior officers followed him. He then went home to Kagoshima where he set about creating a number of sword-fighting academies. Thus began Takamori's rebellion against the Meiji government that he had fought so hard to install.

Takamori was not alone – over 20,000 samurai flocked to Kagoshima between 1874 and 1877, a matter of grave concern in Tokyo. To head off an insurrection the Meiji navy sent several warships to empty Kagoshima's arsenals. But upon hearing this news, the samurai of Kagoshima launched their own preemptive strike by raiding the arsenals and occupying them.

These reports reached Takamori while he was on a hunting trip some distance from Kagoshima. It was never clear if Takamori had planned a revolt against Tokyo, but now, like it or not, he was the leader of one. He rushed back to Kagoshima and prepared his men for war. What followed was a six-month conflict known as the Satsuma Rebellion. On one side was the new national army, 300,000 uniformed soldiers armed with howitzers, Gatling guns, modern rifles and observation balloons. Opposing them were about 40,000 battle-ready samurai who had been training for three years for such a conflict and were ready to fight for the preservation of their class. From the beginning Takamori's army fought like brave samurai warriors of old, but their army was outnumbered and outgunned by the imperial troops. Between February and September Takamori suffered a number of disastrous defeats, and the number of his men fell from thousands to just hundreds.

Facing page: Emperor Meiji is shown marching with his imperial army in 1900. Elements of the samurai ethos often emerged during Japanese conflicts of the twentieth century.

Last Charge of the Samurai

Takamori's last stand took place at the Battle of Shiroyama on 24 September 1877. Here on Shiroyama Hill overlooking Kagoshima, Takamori's last force of 300 men were surrounded by the Imperial Army, which dug trenches, built walls and set up artillery positions to ensure the rebels could not escape. Japanese warships further harassed the rebels by shelling Takamori's position from Kagoshima Bay. With dwindling supplies and ammunition, Takamori's situation soon became desperate. Arming his men with bows and arrows and telling them to draw their swords, Takamori ordered the last charge of the samurai. For a moment it looked as though his strategy had worked. Takamori's samurai charged forward and many crashed into the ranks of rifle-carrying infantry, who had not been trained to fight with a sword or defend themselves against a samurai wielding one. But in the end the modern weaponry won out. Takamori's men were mown down by rifle-fire and Takamori himself was left crippled by a bullet. In death Takamori stayed loyal to the bushidō code and ensured his place as a samurai legend: he had fought bravely, gone down in a blaze of glory and now readied himself for seppuku. As the sword of his second came down, Takamori and the caste known as the samurai breathed their last.

Glossary

ashigaru
Foot soldiers, or skirmishers, most often men who fought on foot.

bakufu
Literally meaning 'tent government', this term describes three warrior governments of Japan: the Kamakura (1185–1333), Muromachi or Ashikaga (1338–1573) and Tokugawa (1603–1867) regimes. A shōgun, or 'barbarian-subduing generalissimo', headed each bakufu.

gekokujō
A term describing the lower conquering the higher, which was often used to describe the 'Warring States' turmoil of the sixteenth century.

hanzei
Reference to a law passed in 1351, whereby half of a province's revenue was earmarked for the procurement of provisions and military supplies.

hara-ate
The simplest type of armour that merely protected the chest and stomach.

haramaki
A type of armour fastened in the side, which represented a simplified version of 'great armour.'

hatsumuri
Gear that covered the forehead and the sides of the face, but not the jaw and neck, that was commonly used through the thirteenth century.

hiya
Primitive three-barrelled guns.

hō-ate
Face guards designed to protect the neck and lower face from arrow wounds, which were adopted as a result of the endemic warfare of the fourteenth century.

ichimaibari uchidashidō
Armour of the sixteenth century made of two large plates of metal, one protecting the torso and the other the back.

kabuto
A steel helmet.

karimata
Two-pronged arrowheads, often used for hunting.

kanjō
Written commendations or documents of praise written by commanders to their followers from 1333 onward.

katana
A curved sword exceeded 0.6m (2ft) in length. Varied slightly from a tachi sword. Became a marker of samurai status in the sixteenth century.

kote
Chain metal gloves designed to protect the upper hands and arms of the samurai.

kuwagata
Two horns located on the helmet of high-ranking warriors. These were thought to provide protection for its wearer.

naginata
A weapon with a long curved blade attached to a wooden staff.

Nanbandō
Japanese armour that used fragments of European armour, most commonly the breast plate, combined with Japanese cloves. Somewhat resembled ichimaibari uchidashidō.

nobushi
Also known as nobuseri, this word refers to skirmishers of all social rank, and not as a 'class' of foot soldiers, as been sometimes assumed. These skirmishers were generally archers, and were indicative of the nature of fighting during the

fourteenth century, when loosely scattered groups of soldiers predominated.

ōdachi

A long sword, otherwise known as a nodachi, or 'field sword', over 0.9m (3ft) in length, which appearing first in the thirteenth century and gained great popularity in the fourteenth. Increasing to 2.1m (7ft) in length, these swords were ideally suited for the scattered battles of the fourteenth century, but were replaced by pikes in the fifteenth and sixteenth centuries as tactics shifted towards massed groups of infantrymen.

ōyoroi

Initially known only as yoroi, this term refers to the most expensive armour, which was worn with shoulder boards (sode), helmets and all other accoutrements. By far the most expensive armour, ōyoroi was made for generals or other high-ranking individuals. This box-like armour was best suited for use on horseback and most effective in protecting against arrows.

shōgun

An eighth-century office, originally designed to quell barbarians, and hence known as sei-i-taishōgun, this post became important as the highest authority within the bakufu, which contained delegated powers of military and judicial authority. Minamoto Yoritomo was appointed to this post in 1192, but he does not appear to have emphasized this office. During the late thirteenth and early fourteenth centuries, the post of shogun was reserved for court nobles, or princes of imperial blood. With the downfall of the Kamakura bakufu in 1333, Ashikaga Takauji started laying claim to the post again, and was appointed shogun in 1338. In 1603, Tokugawa Ieyasu received this position, thereby legitimating his family's dominance, which lasted until 1868.

sode

Armour shoulder boards, covering the upper arms of warriors and used to protect the sides of warriors from arrows as they fought on horseback. Sode, best thought of as attachable shields, continued to be used only as long as warriors fought on horseback.

sugake

An x-shaped weave that was preferred in later styles of armour for it used less braiding.

sune-ate

Shin guards.

tachi

A sword. During the fourteenth century long-swords and, to a lesser extent, naginata were the preferred weapons for hand-to-hand combat. Nevertheless, the bow remained the dominant weapon throughout the fourteenth century. Varied slightly from the more curved blade of a katana.

taishō

A general, appointed from the ranks of noted families on a provisional basis. With the fall of the Kamakura bakufu, most generals were either collaterals of the Ashikaga lineage, imperial princes or court nobles. Their powers were formidable, but rarely institutionalized. Although taishō proved more capable of mobilizing troops than shugo, after the hanzei edicts of 1351 shugo could more effectively wield military force because they could systematically provision their armies.

tantō

Short swords and daggers, under 30cm (1ft) in length.

teppō

A word that initially described explosive projectiles, but later came to be a common term for guns, particularly Portuguese arquebuses.

tōsei gusoku

Simplified armour with minimal weaving that became common in the sixteenth century.

wakizashi

A short curved sword, generally from 0.3–0.6m (1–2ft) in length.

yari

Pikes.

yokohagidō

Metal armor made from horizontal pieces of metal welded together.

Bibliography

Berry, Mary Elizabeth. *Hideyoshi* (Harvard University Press, 1982)

Bryant, Anthony J. *The Samurai* (Osprey, 1989)

Clearly, Thomas. *Training the Samurai Mind: A Bushidō Sourcebook* (Shambhala Publications, 2009)

Clements, Jonathan. *A Brief History of the Samurai* (Constable & Robinson, 2010)

Knoblock, John and Riegel, Jeffrey. *The Annals of Lu Buwei* (Stanford University Press, 2001)

McCullough, Helen Craig. *Taiheiki: A Chronicle of Medieval Japan* (Columbia University Press, 1959)

Musashi, Miyamoto. *The Book of Five Rings* [Downloaded as free text from https://archive.org/]

Nitobe, Inazo. *Bushidō: the Soul of Japan* [Downloaded as free text from https://archive.org/]

Norman, F. J. *The Fighting Man of Japan* (Dover Publications, 2006)

Rankin, Andrew. *Seppuku: A History of Samurai Suicide* (Kodansha International Ltd., 2011)

Sadler, A. L. *Heike Monogatari* (Asiatic Society of Japan, 1918)

Sansom, George. *A History of Japan, 1334–1615 & 1615–1867* (Stanford University Press, 1961)

Sinclaire, Clive. *Samurai: The Weapons and Spirit of the Japanese Warrior* (Salamander Books, 2001)

Truman, Benjamin C. *The Field of Honor* [Downloaded as free text from https://archive.org/]

Tsunetomo, Yamamoto. *Hagakure: The Way of the Samurai* [Downloaded as free text from https://archive.org/]

Turnbull, Stephen. *Samurai: A Military History* (Osprey, 1977)

Turnbull, Stephen. *The Samurai Sourcebook* (Cassell, 1998)

Wilson, William Scott. *The Lone Samurai: The Life of Miyamoto Musashi* (Shambhala Publications, 2013)

Index

Picture Credits